This moving book can chan  s
how we can change ours   s
shoes, find love not fear, an   Ə
sparkling diversity of life's   ⁀.
It is an added teaching tool helping us go further with cultural
empathy, on our own or with our students.

Ruth Richards, MD, PhD
Faculty, Saybrook University
McLean Hospital and Harvard Medical School
Editor, *Everyday Creativity and New Views of Human Nature*

This book defines humanness. It embraces every aspect of life: the
joy of parenting; the sorrow of parenting; the horror of war and
intergenerational trauma; eating disorders and aging; privilege and
second class citizenship. I wanted more.

Regina Walter, 4th Judicial District County Court Judge,
El Paso County, Colorado
Co-chair, Educating Children of Color Summit

Stay Awhile is a safe place where you will want to open yourself up to
the possibilities for connection. You will laugh, cry, and genuinely be
moved by the honesty contained within these pages. The poems
bring to light the inherent subjectivity of our diverse human race in
ways that are sensitive, inspiring, and phenomenological. The gravity
of the poems is immediately apparent and it is magical to be
welcomed into such deep, personal lessons that transcend the
intersubjectivities that too often separate us.

Stay Awhile is an offering of love, of promise, of the truth-
telling that is integral to healing on this journey called life. It is a
demonstration of the type of empathy required for understanding
those things we have not always experienced ourselves. The poets'
voices are simultaneously unique and similar, personal and political.
This collection is for everyone.

Geneva Reynaga-Abiko, PhD
Director, Counseling Services
California Polytechnic State University, San Luis Obispo

Stay Awhile is a collection of poignant "real life" poems written by culturally diverse psychologists, students of psychology, and other poets attuned to the human condition about their "encounters and struggles" arising from just being different. The poems are inspirational and educational for raising consciousness on cultural and diversity issues. The poets speak from their hearts, and the poems require listening with your hearts.

Krishna Kumar, PhD
Professor, West Chester University of Pennsylvania
President, Society for Humanistic Psychology
(American Psychological Association, Division 32)

The teaching, training, and practice of clinical psychology throughout the United States has become overly rigid, narrow, and scientistic. This landmark book is an important counter to that dehumanizing trend and seeks to restore the richness and depths of diverse cultural experiences—with a respectful, empathic honoring of our collective struggles and suffering towards our potential for communal healing and growth. Many of the contributors are psychologists and therapists who, as a consequence of their forays into the lifeworlds of their clients, have been touched and sensitized to the hurt and hopelessness of discrimination, prejudice, and exclusion. By listening to the marginalized and neglected voices among us, as *Stay Awhile* does, we can come together in the spirit of renewed understanding of our shared pain. Then, we can work to rebuild our relationship with the world, and set a more loving and compassionate example for future generations. We owe the contributors of this book a debt of gratitude for sharing the depths of their souls, their courage in vulnerability, their strength to persevere, and their hope for a more just appreciation of the full spectrum of our humanity.

Shawn Rubin, PsyD
Chair, School of Clinical Psychology, Saybrook University
Editor, *Journal of Humanistic Psychology*

Stay Awhile:
Poetic Narratives on Multiculturalism and Diversity

By
Louis Hoffman
&
Nathaniel Granger, Jr.

University
PROFESSORS PRESS

Stay Awhile: Poetic Narratives on Multiculturalism and Diversity
By Louis Hoffman and Nathaniel Granger, Jr.

First Published in 2015, University Professors Press.

ISBN 13: 978-1-939686-08-4

University Professors Press
Colorado Springs, CO
www.universityprofessorspress.com

Front Cover Image by Ted Mallory
Cover Design by Laura Ross

Dedications

I dedicate this book to my three sons: Lakoda, Lukaya, and Lyon, who have inspired many of these poems as they have inspired my life. You have helped me see the world in a different way and motivated me to never give up trying to make it better, so that you may have a better world in which to live. I dedicate this to you with all my love.

~ Louis Hoffman

This book is in dedication to my three gems: My Ruby, Diamond, and Pearl: Nathan Alexander, Stephen Lawrence, and Aliya Janai, who have enriched my life in ways which are invaluable, and continuously inspire me to "Be" and allow me into their worlds and remain open to understanding my world through unconditional love and storytelling.

~ Nathaniel Granger, Jr.

Table of Contents

Acknowledgements

First and foremost, we would like to thank the many poets who contributed poems to this volume. Reading through these poems has heartened and inspired us. These contributions are more than just poems; they are gifts. These poems display heart and compassion, wounds and scars, and amazing resilience and insight. We would also like to thank those who submitted poems that we were not able to accept. We received a wide range of poems and it was difficult for us to not include some of the poems that we, in the end, decided we could not include in this volume. A big note of appreciation goes out to Michael Moats. Michael helped us review poems, but also supported the process of developing the book and contributed one of his own poems. A man with a huge heart, great compassion, and much wisdom, we deeply appreciate Michael's presence in this book and in our lives as a friend and colleague. We also would like to express appreciation for Shawn Rubin, who offered expert editorial assistance in reviewing the manuscript. Finally, we would like to acknowledge Theopia Jackson for her incisive Preface, and Alexandro José Gradilla for his thoughtful and elegant Foreword. Both of these serve as significant contributions to the book that helped us frame the conversation.

I (Louis) often find that the acknowledgement section is one of the most meaningful parts of the book to write. Everything I have ever written feels dependent upon so many people who have encouraged, supported, and cared for me. Without acknowledging these people, the book would not feel complete. As I humbly try to offer my acknowledgments, I would like to begin with my frequent collaborator, Nathaniel Granger. We have worked on many projects through the years with more in the works, but this is one of the most meaningful. My first thought of this book came when listening to Nathaniel bring to life one of his poems through a live reading. I hope that many who read this book will someday also have the opportunity to hear Nathaniel read one of his poems. His gifts of wisdom and speech are inspiring. Nathaniel is a greatly valued friend and colleague who has helped me to grow personally and professionally. It is meaningful beyond words to collaborate with Nathaniel on this project.

When I returned to writing poetry a little over 10-years ago after a long break, I never dreamed that I would ever share my poems beyond a few friends. Yet, the support and encouragement I received when sharing poems with my brother, John Hoffman, and dear friends, Brittany Garrett-Bowser and Robert Murney, gave me the courage to keep writing and begin sharing my poems. I also owe deep appreciation to Saybrook University, which provided a supportive academic environment to integrate poetry and psychology. While few academic institutions would look favorably on such a pursuit, at Saybrook it is a natural fit. I would also like to acknowledge my colleague and friend Dan Hocoy, who designed a new format of classes called "Project X" courses and encouraged me with developing my first course on poetry (Poetry, Healing, and Growth) as well as my poetry and scholarship in general. Students who have taken this course, through their writing and stories, have inspired this project as well. My friend and colleague Steven Pritzker (Director of Saybrook University's Creativity Studies Specialization), who has frequently provided encouragement of my poetry and scholarship, also deserves recognition. I want to thank my colleague Theopia Jackson, who has been courageous in her feedback and consistent with friendship, support, and encouragement. My good friend Shawn Rubin, too, has been consistent in friendship and encouragement and deserves much gratitude. Last, I owe deep gratitude to my family, who have consistently supported my writing, including my parents, Clarence and Lynn Hoffman; brother, John Hoffman; sister-in-law and contributor to this volume, Joy Hoffman; and mother-in-law and fellow poet, Helen Rahming. The first book of poetry that I ever wrote was a hand-written book of poems for my wife, Heatherlyn. She has brought so much beauty to my life that I could not help but turn some of it into poetry. She has often inspired and supported my poetry, and the rest of the time tolerated me when I have been distracted or consumed by a poem trying to form in my thoughts. Several of the poems in this volume were inspired by my sons: Lakoda, Lukaya, and Lyon. My three sons have filled my life with love and poetry, and for this I am deeply thankful.

I (Nathaniel) would like to take a moment to humbly express my heartfelt appreciation to all who have invited me into your "home" through the sharing of your story and contributing to this project by submitting a poem, an encouraging word, or a warm thought. It is through such encounters a connectedness with humanity is fostered. Additionally, I appreciate my enumerable friends and colleagues, specifically Dr. Michael Moats, who has facilitated a phenomenological approach to maintaining a lasting friendship (more often than not, over a cup of Starbucks or an early morning breakfast at the Omelet Parlor), by being courageous to the extent of risking my access into his world and a willingness in understanding my worldview through the use of storytelling. In fact, the poem titled "Cereal Milk" in this volume is dedicated to my friend Michael Moats who, while at my kitchen island collaborating on our book relative to Race and Relationship, paused to drink with me a strawberry-flavored Boost Protein Shake, to which he exclaimed, "This tastes like FrankenBerry Cereal Milk!" We laughed; something we've come to recognize as an integral part of any relationship.

Every journey begins with a single step. A special salute of gratitude goes to my wife, Areta D. Granger, who was part of my beginning and has remained my primary friend and significant support for over a quarter century. Without whom, I would not know the benefit of unconditional love. And, without whom, I would not know the joy of perhaps my life's greatest inspiration, my three children: Nathan, Stephen, and Aliya. Additionally, it is with appreciation to the one who literally facilitated in the taking of my first step, my mother, Margaret (Conaway) Granger, who is an avid reader, from whom I learned to "call it as I see it" and that believing in one's self and "standing up for what one believes" would be a determining factor in life as to whether or not I might procure a relative peace of mind. Thank you Mom for making us read the encyclopedias when we came home from school! Last, but certainly not least, my utmost gratitude goes to Louis Hoffman for his scholarly dexterity, untiring support, and pervasive friendship that has allowed me to burgeon on this journey in ways I never imagined. A godsend. I love you and will forever cherish your belief in me especially during the dark times when the meandering road of this life's journey seemed impossible to travel.

For relationship sake, it behooves us to learn the beauty of storytelling. It is the one thing that will assist in the understanding of how others view their worlds and react to them, and help us to resist the temptation of telling others how they should react and behave toward their worlds! Others' worldviews may be very different from our own, but they are based on perceptions, which are the substrata of their "realities." It is our reality that determines how we feel, think, and be.

Preface

"There is no greater agony than bearing an untold
story inside you."
~ Maya Angelou

It is an extreme honor to be invited to draft this Preface for such a
powerfully therapeutic healing resource. Aptly noted, the poems
gathered here should be of interest to many. Yet, as a clinical
psychologist-of-color engaged in the training of future healers, I am
always struck by colleagues and clinicians-in-training commenting
on not knowing how to talk about multiculturalism in its many
varieties, from sexual orientation to gender to race and ethnicity. We
are all multicultural. It is no surprise that we simply need to step out
of our professional boundaries or comfort-zone and step into the
humanities, the wholeness of ourselves. Louis Hoffman and
Nathaniel Granger, Jr. have brilliantly brought together the voices of
our souls, explicating what it means to be fully human and engaged. I
am intrigued by the diversity of titles and appreciate the
multicultural quilt of experiences. Sample the spices of *I Am the
Terrorist, The Virtues of Big Brother, I Don't Want to Hate Being a
Mother, The Skin You're In, Longing for the Reclamation of the De-
colonized Indigenous Mind,* and *Revelations* to name a few. I am in
awe of the conversations within and across selves that are to emerge
from those touched by the stories embedded here. It is my prayer
that this bed of poetic justice voices will continue to fuel and nourish
those of us who are diligently seeking to illuminate the inner
strength of our collective multiculturalism. More specifically, I invite
each of you to curl up on a courageous couch with a warm blanket of
self-awareness, a cup of curiosity, and be fully present for
transformative refreshments... indulge yourself!

Theopia Jackson, PhD
Faculty, Saybrook University
Site Training Coordinator, Department of Psychiatry
UCSF Benioff Children's Hospital Oakland

Foreword

After reading the innovative collection of poems, *Stay Awhile: Poetic Narratives on Multiculturalism and Diversity* by Louis Hoffman and Nathaniel Granger, Jr. I am reminded that the ancient Greek *poiēsis* is root of the modern word poetry. *Poiēsis* meant "formation" or "to make." More accurately, this collection reflects what philosophers referred to as "autopoiesis," which refers to self-maintaining or self-constructing living systems. Furthermore, this collection of poetry also reminds us that in all ancient societies poetry was seen as the purest and most dangerous form of truth and knowledge. Without a doubt Hoffman and Granger succeed at pulling together a wide array of scholar-poets who write about the living systems of multiculturalism and diversity. All of the poets touch on the themes that writing poetry is one of the most intimate forms of self-writing or an act of auto-ethnography. The poets in this collection write of vast experiences of diversity not as etched in stone, but as living, breathing process that must be constantly attended to.

Some examples of the poetic works include Nathaniel Granger Jr.'s poem "'Dat 'Dere Book," which goes back in time to a period where knowledge and literacy were seen as a threat to the prosperous institution of slavery. For readers who are unaware of this history there is no way to understand the current struggle for knowledge, education, and justice within the African American community, or why schooling and access to integrated schools was at the heart of the Civil Rights Movement. In a transnational moment within the collection, Nesreen Alsoraimi's "Palestinian Mamma" challenges the false representation uttered by Golda Meir that enunciated "Peace will come when the Arabs will love their children more than they hate us." The intersection of "Palestinian," "woman," "refuge," and "mother" in this current and historical context demonstrates the active role that women play within families and communities. This is also a counter-narrative to the idea of Arab women as objects or docile beings. In another piece that speaks the transnational and local experience of dis-location, trauma, and dis-identification is "No Place to Land" by Veronica Lac. This poem is not about despair, but about optimism because one way or another we are all "impure" hybrids, which is key to the human condition. The collection concludes with the poignant powerful poem, "We Are

More," by Dakota Gundy. In this lyrical narrative Gundy lays out a
powerful manifesto of reclaiming humanity and inventing a new
"universality" based on inclusion and celebrating difference.

The collection is pedagogically sound as well. Embedded in
the collection are themes that help guide the reader and the
instructor. Themes include Cultural Empathy, Responding to
Prejudice and Discrimination, Identity, Parenthood and Family,
Humor, Encounters with Other Cultures, Self Reflection, Historical
Reflection, Activism, Communication, Finding One's Voice, Healing,
and Hope. The editors include various lesson plans in order to help
instructors connect these themes with the experiences of their
students. This collection embodies the best traditions and practices
put forth by Paulo Freire, who reminded us that true social change
cannot occur unless there is responsibility, love, and hope. *Stay
Awhile* will open minds and hearts.

Alexandro José Gradilla, PhD
Associate Professor and Chair
Chicana and Chicano Studies Department
California State University, Fullerton

Introduction

This is not your typical poetry book, and this is by design with full intentionality. The idea for this book emerged organically. For several years, we have been presenting together and writing together on the topic of multiculturalism in the academic field of psychology. Throughout this time, both of us were also engaged in poetry and the arts, which we each integrated into our scholarly work. It was often the poetic words more than the finely tuned scholarship that impacted people the most deeply and brought forth conversations leading to more significant change.

Along with the words of appreciation for the poems and other art forms we shared, we would occasionally receive poems and other artistic expressions from those who heard us talk or read our writing. These were incredible gifts. From this, we decided to offer a workshop on Using Art to Facilitate Cultural Empathy at the Society for Humanistic Psychology Hospitality Suite at the Annual Convention of the American Psychological Association. It was in preparing for this workshop that we decided to develop *Stay Awhile*.

We could have approached the book by seeking to collect a volume of previously published poems that focused on multiculturalism and diversity; however, this was not our interest. We wanted poems that emerged from every day experience. Most of the poems in this book were not contributed by professional poets or individuals who have previously sought to publish or share their poetry. This, we believe, is part of the power and beauty of this volume. The poems are real accounts of encounters and struggles. These poems are real life.

In seeking and reviewing poems, we were intentional about including poems that reflect various different styles of poetry. Within these pages you will find poems ranging from Haiku to prose poetry. Some of the styles of poems may not fit with what is traditionally considered poetry. This reflects an appreciation for the diverse ways in which one can approach poetry. We did, however, show a preference for poems that were accessible and poems where the diversity themes were evident. While this could be criticized from an artistic perspective, we believed it was important for our goals for the book. By focusing on poems that, for the most part, are more accessible poems, the result is a poetry book that will appeal to more than just scholars of poetry. This is a book for anyone interested in multiculturalism and diversity.

An Invitation

One of the most notable aspects of the human condition is that of diversity and multiculturalism. If ever an understatement, the old adage "No two people are alike" is indubitable. No other creature can possess as many differences within its species and still belong to that same species as with *homo sapiens.* Around the world today, some 7,000 distinct languages are spoken. That's 7,000 different ways of saying "stay awhile"—more languages in one species of mammal than there are mammalian species. What's more, these 7,000 languages probably make up just a fraction of those ever spoken in our history. To put human linguistic diversity into perspective, you could take a gorilla or chimpanzee from its troop and plop it down anywhere these species are found, and it would know how to communicate. You could repeat this with donkeys, crickets, or goldfish and get the same outcome. However, humans, more often that not, cannot or do not relate fully with one another because of diversity. The beauty of our multiculturalism perpetuates the ugliness of our separateness. The primary caveat lending itself to this division is in the failure to understand one another through the simplicity of storytelling. Camus once said, "Man is the only creature who refuses to be what he is." Whenever a person closes himself or herself off from listening to another's story, he or she is in essence saying, "I refuse to get to know you for who you really are" or "In my eyes, I cannot accept you for who you really are." Nonetheless, when one engages in the sharing of stories, he or she is proverbially saying, "Welcome into my home," and in fact, "Stay awhile."

While working on my (Nathaniel) Masters Degree in Counseling and Human Services, one of the most intriguing and interactive classes was a class that focused on multicultural competencies in therapy. The class itself was relatively diverse with students from different racial and cultural backgrounds. The content of the class was fantastic in that it discussed diversity and how it could impact the therapeutic relationship both negatively and positively. It spoke of the importance of respect for and appreciation of differences in ethnicity, gender, age, national origin, disability, sexual orientation, education, and religion. However, what I found superlative were the relationships formed by deciding to meet for classes away from the campus, outside the sterility of the classroom, in different homes. It was in the storytelling in the homes that relationships formed that transcend cultural barriers. One relationship in particular, I will forever remember. Shannon, a young White woman, found much joy when hosting the "class session" at her parents' home. Her eyes would always fill with a tearful glee at the listening of a poem or story. Certainly, Shannon's jaw would hurt due to excessive smiling. Nearing time for graduation, Shannon, along with another friend, Carolyn, was fatally injured in a car accident. I was asked to give remarks at Shannon's Memorial Service to which I simply recalled Shannon's words whenever it came time to leave her home: "Stay awhile. Have another glass of wine."

This book is an invitation into our homes. In our home, we fight, forgive, laugh, and love. You will find upon accepting the invitation into our home that we find humor as in the poem "Against Diversity." In our home, we are safe to discuss the uncomfortable issues of sexual orientation, as found in "Bi The Way," and parenting, as engaged in "My Imperfect Perfect Son." Take your shoes off, and share in the historical trauma of "Dat 'Dere Book," and the stories relative to ethnicity as in "Climbing Sacramento Street in San Francisco." In our home, you will note that we are passionate, yet safe to share our feelings relative to activism as in "What I Fear" and "I Am the Terrorist." At the end of the day, in our home, you are on the "Road to Mend" where you will find healing, and find hope in "Someday." We ask that you will make yourself at home, and once the hour is late and you feel as if you have overextended your welcome, "Stay Awhile."

A Book to Be Used

We hope *Stay Awhile* will be appreciated for its artistic contribution; however, we also hope that this book will be used to promote change—personally and at a social level. We are both teachers and therapists, and we deeply believe that poems can be used in the service of learning, healing, and growth. To encourage *Stay Awhile* as something that can be used, we have included a discussion of important themes that we saw emerge in the poems as we read through them. Also, at the end of the book we have included an Appendix with activities that can be used in conjunction with this book. We hope that this book will find its way into classrooms, group discussions, and many other settings over time.

As you read these poems—whether curled up by yourself with a warm cup of coffee, in a small group, or in a classroom—we hope that with each poem you will stay awhile. Before intellectually interpreting the poem, sit with it—stay awhile. Imagine how it would feel to write this poem. Imagine the voice of this poem being your own voice. Feel the poem. Then consider what you can learn from the poem. When we do not engage poems openly and stay awhile with them, it is easy to miss the deeper meanings and callings of the poem.

Themes

As noted, a number of important themes emerged as we read and reread these poems. These themes can help illuminate the ways that poetry can be used to facilitate dialogues, healing, growth, insight, and deeper awareness of diversity. Many of the poems reflect several of these themes. Certainly, the list of themes that we identified is not comprehensive and we would not want to use these themes to put poems in a box that could limit them. Yet, we hope reflecting upon these themes will help readers consider ways that this book and these poems can be used.

Cultural Empathy

Poems often emerge from very personal experiences. They give a glimpse inside the private thoughts and experiences of the poet. As such, poetry can serve to promote empathy. The poems in this book show at least two ways that poetry can facilitate empathy. First, the poems give an insight into personal experience that is not easily conveyed in a direct narrative. For example, "Palestinian Mamma" facilitates empathy on two levels. First, it shows the author deepening her own empathy for her Mamma, while at the same time tells a personal story of suffering that brings understanding to a particular cultural experience.

Second, the process of writing poetry can be used to deepen empathy. For instance, the poem "I'll Drink to Judgment" was written about the experience of homelessness and represents Socioeconomic Status (SES) as a form of diversity. This poem was written in the voice of someone who is homeless; however, the author never himself experienced being homeless. The inspiration came through listening to many stories of people experiencing homelessness while in the role of a psychologist. The process of writing this poem helped deepen empathy for the struggle and suffering of people experiencing homelessness.

Responding to Prejudice and Discrimination

There is no one right way to respond to prejudice and discrimination. More often than not, individuals may need to respond on multiple levels: processing their hurt, pain, and anger; trying to understand where the offending person is coming from and if they were intentional in their offense; and confronting the offense. Poetry can help respond to prejudice and discrimination in many ways. It can help to heal the wounds caused. It can help to understand the other person. It can be a way of confronting prejudice and discrimination. It can be a way of using the hurt to inspire change.

In "Why I Have Grown to Hate Dolls," the reader witnesses a journey through recognizing the experience of sexism to finding one's voice. The poem reflects different layers of the emotional experience – the hurt, the pain, the questioning. In the end, there is a strength that is conveyed in the poem; a strength even in owning one's anger. The poem pays witness to a transformation and, in just one poem, reflects responding on multiple levels.

Identity

Identity is one of the most common themes in this book. This is seen in the struggle to find one's identity as bisexual and bi-cultural; coming to terms with living in a culture seemingly far from the culture where one was born; and coming to terms with an identity of being privileged or an ally. For example, Paul Wong's "Climbing Sacramento Street in San Francisco" powerfully reflects upon a longing for one's homeland and a pondering of what it means to be living in a culture so different from one's culture of origin.

Other poems reflect upon a different identity struggle that emerges from experiencing microaggressions, prejudice, and discrimination. For some, their identity was shaken by these experiences. The poems tell the story of journeying through one's questioning and struggle before reclaiming one's identity, maybe in a slightly different form due to these painful experiences.

Parenthood and Family

Similar to the struggles with personal identity are the familial struggles, which often reflect a broader conception of identity, especially for cultures that maintain a form of collectivist identity. Several poems reflect this intersection of personal and collective identity, particularly in the role of a parent. For instance, "My Imperfect Perfect Son" speak to the challenges and terror that can be associated with raising an African American son in a world where stories like that of Trayvon Martin and Michael Brown seem all to commonplace.

Humor
Humor, when used appropriately, can be a wonderful teacher. Although it is difficult to use humor around an issue as sensitive as diversity, there are a few poems in this volume that use humor very well. For example, Tom Greening is well known for his use of humor in poetry to make some rather profound statements and insights. Both of his poems included in this volume use a touch of humor, but also speak powerfully to an underlying lesson. For some, the disarming of the humor helps to look more honestly at underlying reality.

Encounters with Other Cultures
Several poems in this volume speak to multiculturalism more subtly in the form of encountering a different culture. As the poet uses poetry to reflect upon such encounters, there is often a sense of appreciation, wonderment, insight, or even awe. Cultivating an appreciation and openness to difference can be a powerful form of cultural healing.

"Breaking My Snow Globe" is a poem that reflects growth and transformation through experiencing another culture. In reading the poem, one can journey with the author to understanding. The poem uses wonderful imagery to paint a picture of some of her experiences. In the end, the poem testifies that the author did not just visit another culture; she encountered it.

Self-Reflection
Poems can be an effective form of self-reflection, or looking inside oneself to discover truths about oneself and the world. Several poems in this volume illustrate this theme of self-reflection. The poems "Revelation" and "Face of Privilege" are self-reflections about White privilege. It is not easy to be a multicultural ally. While the struggles of being an ally pale in comparison to the struggles of facing prejudice, microaggressions, and discrimination more

directly, it still takes courage to stand up and be an ally. The process of self-refection can help maintain this courage.

Historical Reflection

Microaggressions, prejudice, and discrimination have deep roots in history. The wounds of today are intimately intertwined with historical trauma. Poems such as "'Dat 'Dere Book" speak to these histories with the potential to deepen understanding and empathy. "The Rage of Age" takes a different approach to considering history through recognizing that so much of the hurt and anger of now cannot be separated from the suffering of then.

Activism

A number of poems reflect a call for change or a call for activism. For instance, two poems refer to the death of Trayvon Martin and the subsequent trial of George Zimmerman as inspiration. These poems directly or indirectly call for people to stand up and demand change. Through these poems, tribute is paid to those whose sacrifices and suffering serve to inspire others to make a positive change in the world. Similarly, the poem "I Am the Terrorist" was written as a response to a disturbingly insensitive, even hostile, statement about a religious group. In a tone that reflects deep pain as well as anger, the poem cries out for the pain of people who have experienced such hatred. While this poem could also be seen as encouraging empathy for the victims of such intense prejudice and discrimination, the tone seems to speak more forcefully to that of an activist's call for change.

Activist poems carry a risk. These poems often can easily be misunderstood, as is the case with "I Am the Terrorist." Yet, if we are not willing to accept the risk associated with taking a stand, it is not likely that we will ever be able to make a difference in the world. The safe route is too often impotent. Any time we engage in dialogues about diversity, we are engaging in risk. To be an activist is to take that risk thoughtfully and knowingly. Unfortunately, activism is often solely associated with anger and passion; however, the best activism is rooted in empathy, self-reflection, and openness.

Communication

Through years of researching, teaching, writing, and presenting about multiculturalism and diversity, we have often encountered people who have felt stuck in trying to learn how to communicate about diversity. Many potential allies, who in their heart are committed to diversity, have avoided taking on the role of being an ally for fear of being misunderstood or not knowing how to communicate in a sensitive manner with language and vocabulary that will be accepted.

At other times, microaggressions, which are subtle and often unintentional forms of prejudice, are evident in the language used, yet easily denied. Several poems, such as Dan Hocoy's "Clear Communication," reflect such communication challenges.

Finding One's Voice

Traveling through the dark valleys of scars and wounds of prejudice and discrimination is not easy. It is easy to lose oneself in the shadows of this journey. Finding one's voice can be a powerful way of bringing light and meaning to this painful journey. Many poems in this volume reflect finding ones voice, often through the journey of the poem itself. "I am a Girl" speaks to finding one's voice and being okay with it. There is strength in the statement, "I am a Girl." It should not take strength and courage to make this statement, yet, many who have been wounded by how girls and women are treated face this struggle. Maybe reading "I am a Girl"—even reading it out loud—can be a way of asserting one's voice.

Healing

A primary reason that we both have been drawn to poetry is the recognition that poetry holds tremendous power for healing. Before there was psychotherapy, there was poetry, which can be recognized as one of the oldest healing arts that has been utilized across many different cultures throughout history. Today, some professionals speak of poetry therapy, and sometimes this is mistaken as something new and innovative. However, while there are many new and innovative ways of doing poetry therapy, in many ways we could say that poetry therapy is really an indigenous approach to healing that we are just now recognizing and learning to integrate into our contemporary models of healing, such as psychotherapy.

Hope

Poetry often brings inspiration and hope. We use poetry to look into the dark shadows that need to be exposed and we use poetry to share transformative light with the world. Often, when the topic of multiculturalism and diversity comes up, dread and defenses quickly rise as people anticipate tense and conflicted conversations. It is unfortunate that multiculturalism and diversity, which reflect the beauty of this world, has become something that is feared and avoided. Yet, we can reclaim the beauty and hope that is connected to the splendor of our differences. "Making the World Better" is a poem that speaks to hope and change, as well as a way that we can be part of that change. "We are More" is a powerful piece that, in repeating, "We are More," brings a sense of hope and a vision of something more. We were intentional about choosing this for our closing poem. After journeying through poems of questioning and suffering, reflection and recognition, appreciation and feeling misunderstood, "We are More" closes the book and sends us out with a blessing. As your read, "we are more" over and over in this poem, we encourage you to connect with the transformative energy of these three powerful words. Let these words carry all the emotion that has come forth as you read these poems and let these words give direction to these emotions. We are more. We are powerful. We can make a difference. *We will make a difference*—together.

Conclusion

We hope that you are touched and inspired by the poems in *Stay Awhile*, and hope that many of you respond by writing your own poems and your own stories. We invite you to find the Facebook page for *Stay Awhile: Poetic Narratives on Multiculturalism and Diversity* and follow the story of this book and where it may lead—maybe even to subsequent volumes of *Stay Awhile*.

Poems

Shades of Purple
Emily Lasinsky

It's hard to be blue
in a world of red,
where everyone is afraid of becoming purple.
Keep the separation-
don't want to risk the chance that influence may occur.
Afraid of the responsibility that accompanies change.

I'm not afraid to be touched by the red,
to hear stories
that conflict with what I've known.
All these pieces make up the collective whole,
need each other to reach a better understanding,
but we scatter to the familiar and share whispers,
thinking we know who we are.

What if...
We allow ourselves to perceive a beautiful mosaic
   instead of random paint splotches that cover the
   cracks of white walls?
   Instead of desperately striving to tune out the bad, we seek the
      good?
   Instead of collision, we respect each other enough to
   make a unified decision?

Don't have to always agree,
Don't have to be the same,
but think about what it would be like if for only one day
we could come together in appreciation for the differences and enjoy
the shades of purple-
A peace of heaven.

Making the World Better
Michael Moats

Do not judge those that believe different than you.
Do not cast disparaging remarks.
Your beliefs are oppressive and therefore not tolerated.
So, believe as I do, and the world will be a better place.
Who is speaking?
Who is listening?
Judging those that judge others,
A toxic eddy of sludge being sold as drinking water.
Celebrating diversity as I bash my Christian brothers.
Bringing love to the world by sharing that you are going to Hell.
Monologues in proximity,
Dialogue and relationship are but faint dreams behind heavy armor.
Leading the way to making a better world, full of love.
Not noticing the bodies on which I step
In the pursuit of my enlightened cause.
I shall sleep well tonight in the peace of my actions;
I shall be restless in that I am not understood.

'Dat 'Dere Book
Nathaniel Granger, Jr.

Whatchu doin?! Put 'dat book down!
You's gone git us alls in trouble!
Who learned you how to read anyway?
Miss Paulie?!
You tell Miss Paulie don't she ever learn you how to read no mo'
You's gone git us alls in trouble!
Master said da biggest sin for a negro
Is the sin of learnin'
Master said a negro ain't s'posed to be learned
Master said negroes s'posed to be trained
Just like 'dat scrong mule out back
And like 'dat mare over there
Likes all the other animals on this here plantation.
Master said it's right 'dere in the Good Book.
You's gone git us alls in trouble!
You's be better off sirein' the master's handmaid
Than to git caught readin' from 'dat 'dere book.
My daddy couldn't read
My mammy couldn't read
I's can't read
And I's be damned if I's 'low
One of mine's to read from 'dat 'dere book.
If 'da master don't kill you
I'll kill you myself,
So, help me God!
You's gone git us alls in trouble!
You's gone git us alls in trouble!

Palestinian Mamma
Nesreen Alsoraimi

Mamma
My Palestinian Mamma
Reservoir of
collective trauma
Passer on
of tradition
of pain
of cultural disdain
Cold and icy
Emotion comes with a price
Once, I did not understand
and then I did too well
I dropped myself
then propped myself
fought her and I fought myself
tried to prevent the cycle
from repeating
from secreting
poison in our water
the formation of a daughter
and a mother-to-be
I gently let go for me
and for you mama
I'm saving you the trouble of that choice
That struggle
between them and me
between my need for intimacy and your sanity
I know it's hard
To abandon that bubble
even for a moment
with their eyes on you
watching and judging your every move
Conflicting agendas
sending you reeling from one side to the other
My battle is more mellow
I know
I did not feel the heat of the explosions
I did not experience the sting of such hate

I did not watch those I love
get shot in the head
rot in their beds
malnutritioned and dead
I did not have to flee for my life
Was not abused
Was not outcast....except by you
Now and then
You and him
So now I see
that the sentiment remained
the need to share that pain
You learned both scripts
Trained in the art of war
while love took a back seat
Maybe it's true
That it toughens you up
Strong on the outside
yet weak in between
Bruised fruit
So hard to chew
Relentless roots
War forcing men and women
to take on
what they never asked for
Shifting roles
Paying trolls under bridges
Making deals with the devil
Level after level
of disintegration
of love
of respect for the rights of the weaker
the meeker
to save the institution
of family
of ethnic identity
Men overcompensating
for emasculination
Devastation
of human connection
Detection of emotion

causes confusion
and defensive pride
PRIDE!
Fill in the blank
Higher your rank
boost that esteem
that they buried in the rubble
that they stripped from "your" people
Ridged and crowded with inhibitions
and those wonderful traditions
that hug you
and choke you
that calm you
and provoke you
that also come with a price
That comfort will cost you
maybe your children
or your grown women
Who ask you to swim
face your demons
let go of the friend who helped you through
that crutch
fear of touch
steps of separation
dreams of reparation
belonging and excluding
You are exuding
the only power you have
the power that lasts
your seal of approval
Jeopardizing your sense of order
and what they taught you was moral
It's clashing and smashing
and I know
that this hurt
must be less intimidating
than what would lie beneath
if you ripped off that blindfold
if you let go of that raft
You're afraid
of the darkness

the answerless
self guided
case by case
fluid
body of feelings
Afraid
of being lost at sea

Scream
Paul T. P. Wong

It will never stop, it will never end;
It comes from the depths of desperation,
From the darkest hour of despair,
From a heart breaking into many pieces.
It will scream at the top of one's voice,
A primal scream that goes on and on
Until the pain ends.

I'll Drink to Judgment

Louis Hoffman

They don't know my story
Don't want to, and I
No longer want to tell it

I sit by the fire
My "new" tent is brown
It blends in better than the green
With the grey and brown background
And I just want to blend in to nothingness
My campsite is convenience, not choice
My trees are the streetlights
A spotlight on humiliation
My lake the gutter puddles
That I am ashamed to say
Have been a bath a time or two
The fire is almost out now
I hastily drink so the fear may be gone
Before the flames...
Maybe I'll sleep tonight

Soon they will run us off again
To where I don't know
I'll hide my tent a day or two
Then we'll be back
Always back
Despite the nasty looks as if
To cast their shame on us
It's too far to walk those days
When our campground has been broken
Hard to find a spot I can walk to
Where my can may hear enough jingle
For a meal that's not secondhand
And there is enough light and passer-bys
So that the late night visitors
Are discouraged from coming
Or at least staying too long

They, too, don't want to be seen
For to rob those who have nothing
Is too low even for most criminals

Yesterday some kids kicked my can
As they laughed out loud
I wonder if they were the same ones who
The day before, slipped a note inside:
"Get a job you fuckin' bum"
Once I would have been indignant
Now I just am
As I kept looking to see if a treasure
May have been hidden
Maybe enough to take the edge off

Back when I still held my dignity
I'd proudly tell my shameful story
Even if they didn't ask, I had to tell it
I wasn't "one of them"
I was different
I once, too, had a job
Had dreams, even a family
A shaming look for those who did not
But these all went away
There was no more "them," instead "us"
Sure, I made mistakes, too
But I never chose this life
And never deserved this fate

I used to fight in line at the shelters
Go door to door each day
Hoping for a job
Later, even just work for a day
Then one day a handout would do
After a while no one would hire
Someone unemployed so long
Soon no one would even look at
A man who couldn't afford to shower
I gave in and accepted my destiny
I could barely afford a drink,
And hope cost so much more

At first, I thought,
"Who could blame a man,
For taking a drink on a cold night."
After being robbed and beaten several times
Thrown in the hospital, thrown in jail,
I thought,
"Who could blame a man,
For drinking away a little of the pain."
The needles, too, were tempting
Others fell prey
Some before their destiny took hold,
Others after
But I was too proud
And stopped with the drink
Except that one stormy night
When it was all that could make
The rain and cold go away

In the beginning, I kept the drink hidden
Begging as a homeless person is hard enough
To beg as a drunk is unbearable
But it didn't matter
Everyone assumed the same
I saw the judgment when I took a dollar,
"You're not going to buy a drink, are you?"
I used to honor their wish
But when I misplaced my dignity
No honor was left

Now I drink and don't feel ashamed
Some days, I even ask for a beer
A few laugh as they say,
"I appreciate your honesty."
I laugh with them while they laugh at me
Others just turn away
So I take what I can get
And I'll take what comes with it
The scornful looks, the averted eyes
Yes, judgment
I'll drink to that.

The Virtue of Big Brothers
Candice Hershman

Woman sat down
after she looked into the photograph,
and saw herself
in her big brother's face.

She knew he was a good man.
He was faithful.
He was gentle.
He went out of his way
to make her laugh.
He protected her.

After opening her wounds up
that afternoon,
wrongs she had not forgotten
done to her so many years ago,
today
she was told it should have driven her mad,
something she'd heard by at least three therapists
in her youth,
but it did not drive her mad . . .

These were wrongs she had not forgotten,
but she realized
she had forgotten the pain
and it was still there.
Someone recently
had touched the wound.
It was not malicious.
They didn't know.

She was asked by
her guide
to the center of
her self,
"how did you keep from losing your mind
the way your younger brother did?"

The woman replied:
"I knew how to fight.
I was shamed for it,
but I know it kept me alert,
kept me from leaving this world.
It is my fighting
that kept me alive."

She thought for a minute.
She remembered,
and then she told her:

"My brother taught me how to fight.
He learned Karate and Tae Kwon Do.
He told me that as a girl,
I would be good at Tae Kwon Do
because it is about kicking,
flexibility and use of the legs,
and women have more power
in their legs and hips.
He made me practice kick reps
daily, over and over,
taught me his belt routines,
and made me have sparring matches
with my little brother
in the back yard.
I hated it then.
I didn't like being hit
in a sparring match.
Even my little brother
was burlier than me.
I was a tiny, small boned girl,
and seemed to be frail.
But one day,
a girl wouldn't stop trying
to hurt me,
pushed me into a pile
of broken glass,
and so I jumped up
and kicked her in the face.
I was so tiny,

so shy,
and she was so big and bold,
but she stopped
and she ran away.
I surprised her.
I surprised myself."

"I was always a fighter.
I was ridiculed for it.
I was called "violent"
and "problem child"
for protecting myself.
Now I see,
it kept me
from losing my mind.
At least when I was angry and fighting,
I had not fled my body
like my little brother had fled his."

She thought about
the greatest betrayal
by her mother;
that deep existential wound.
Some people learn earlier,
too early . . .
that the world has a dark side
and will not always protect you.

Then she remembered:

"My big brother protected me.
When there was a serial killer loose
and we were home alone at night
because our mother worked graveyard,
he duct taped a butcher knife
to the end of a broom
and kept it under the sofa bed
in the living room."

"When I was 14,
a girl bullied me
because a boy she liked
liked me instead.
It didn't matter that I didn't like him.
She threatened to beat me up.
My brother
and his leather booted,
motorcycle riding,
chain belted
mohawk friends walked to the school
and waited outside of the classroom
for me.
That girl
never bothered me again."

"When I was 16,
my brother took my first boyfriend aside
and told him
he would break all of his limbs
if he ever hurt me.
He told all of his friends
he would hurt them if they even
considered me.
One did.
Twenty years later,
my brother confronted him."

She paused again.

"I had not forgotten the wrongs,
and I had not forgotten the rights.
I did forget the pain,
and I also forgot
the goodness of my big brother
for always reminding me
to accept nothing less than the best,
for making me laugh and smile,
for keeping my honor,
and most importantly,
for protecting me.

My brother is proof
that good men exist."

She went home.
She walked down the hall
and looked at that smile
in the photograph.
It was the first time she realized,
she looked like her big brother.
Incredibly alike.
She felt proud
to share that face.
That face
probably saved her life.

A Thing of Legos
Amelia Isabel Torres

Legos
Lego
Individual
I

Building
blocks of matter
Unlimited
On my dress
In my chest
A kingdom of legos
Nations of dreams
Creation it seems
is but a thing of legos

Common Language
Tess Crescini

I dreamt you were a poem.
The silence between space and ink, ripe and sweet like sugar cane;
we held hands in places scented like the salty sea.
We have a common language
that float like mists over naked bodies inching, wanting,
cleaving to each other's warmth.

But in my ordinary waking reality,
we have two languages: yours and mine.
Our conversations border at the edge of a rumbling volcano,
desiring to spew out its lava onto the rich dark soil.

Our voices thicken with choice words -
careful, oh so careful, not to give away
vulnerabilities, insecurities.

You read my poems about love, about running out of love.
You grind the words, mix them with uncertainty.
You're an imagining I wish would fill the hole in my heart,
dry my damp face.

Perhaps, I'm only homesick for a place where coconuts thrive,
for a place where I can drink the rain
straight from the clouds.

Check Your Self
Roxanne Christensen

It happened
before I was old enough to know
A Times New Roman
12 point
square
That dared
ask me
to fit inside
its equilateral lines

Am I everything of my blood
brown skin
that always almost fit in?
No more natural heritage
than a book report
or Slumdog story
and a baby
with rosebud mouth
in burlap rags
held by the last hands
that matched her tone
in the arms of countryman and stranger

Am I
White
and finally right
with my university intonation
and my father's debonair vocation
Demurity
Financially secured
despite
my cultural impurity

What of my mother's
thick accent
flowing like honey over buttered bread
on a Persian carpet breakfast
Fierce woman of a man's God-ful land

Gentle teacher
with the softest of hand
English lullaby's in a Farsi cadence
Unmatchable beauty
and eyes of political unrest

I am illogical math
Where one and one made four
And when a native tongue failed me
Music transcends my lacking dialect
Born with not enough words
and too many songs
My heritage is written on my heart
Self emblazoned in my soul

Do I belong to nothing
or am I a part of all
To be everything
must I truly be nothing whole
The sum of parts
sewn from many hearts
betrothed to my role

Am I
blood and objective bone
Learned culture
Present family
Abandoned history
My parents
Now mother
I must live to show
my sweetly cinnamon children
to define self
as far more
than "other."

No Place to Land
Veronica Lac

I see I am otherness to you
as you attempt to place me
categorizing, judging,
baffling that I'm both,
not either or
and more complex
than your experience contains
or allows
leaving me stranded
with no place to land
no hand to hold
No home
No sanctuary
No place to call my own.
No language
No country
No tribe to share my soul.

For us in-betweeners of
mixed race, transnational,
transcultural souls,
pioneers across boundaries
have learnt to pretend
to pass, to fit in and blend,
losing parts of ourselves
along the way
searching for likeness
feeling betrayed,
looking for acceptance
but not alike enough
for either, or.

If only it is understood
that there is no pureness of race, ethnicity,
or culture,
that we are all hybrids,
that the only pureness found is
in our humanity,

then maybe, we can all belong
somewhere,
maybe
we can find our home.

Innocent
Louis Hoffman

My son,
I don't know how
to tell you
As I look in those big, brown
innocent eyes
That you will never be
innocent.

You hair is too
coarse
Your nose, too wide
Your skin, too dark
So that even your love
if too passionate
or maybe not passionate enough
Will stir fear
In those who share
only half
your race

For those who fear you
before
they know you
In every act they will search
and find
evidence
supporting the verdict
already made
Guilt colors the evidence

Guilt justifies the evidence

My son,
I don't know how
to tell you
Those big, brown
innocent eyes.
That big loving heart

They will never know,
They will never allow
for your innocence.

In the Aftermath
Elizabeth Wolfson

In the aftermath of Thanksgiving
three young men throw a football
down from the cliff
at the edge of the house
where the family meal was taken.
Back and forth goes the ball on the beach.
One shouts to his dog, *Ace,*
the other cries "goal!"

Sounds of the fullness
of young lives, past repast.

A perfectly browned turkey leg
on the platter in the kitchen
is leftover from the feast
served up by my firstborn son.
No longer a child,
he has learned less from his mother
about what to do, then what not to do.
Raised on pizza, pasta, and Chinese take-out
he cooks like a pro.

So much to be thankful for
-a turkey at a time.

I think of Margaret last week at "assisted" living, rejoicing
in a pre-Thanksgiving-faux-vegetarian meal
prepared by an invisible chef
for a dining hall of elders
at their last stop.

At ninety two,
eyesight dimmed and steps unsteady
she has razor sharp recall of
Berlin's treacherous streets
and the long hungry days of
hunting for her mother.
The rest, is best forgotten.

In this place of ravaged history
 and diminishing tomorrows,
the faded number on her forearm
is carved onto her bones.
She can recite it backwards, but
cannot recall her daughter's name.
Lifting a shaky fork,
she smiles to no one and gives thanks
that no birds were killed for this meal.

Harold sits in his wheelchair across the way
claiming medals from a great war.
A Filipino caregiver
unfolds a napkin onto his lap with one hand,
checking text messages with the other.
She is oblivious to the robe pocket bulge
of plastic spoons stashed
for the next Depression.

Is this a place of thanks?
This residence of remnants where
my mother now breaks daily bread
oblivious to ammonia smells
amongst all those smooth faces gone wrinkled,
biding time between breakfast, lunch, dinner, and bed,
wisdom of experience bringing no expectation of tomorrow.

All those smiling and vacant eyes
with a story behind them that no one cares to hear,
hours ahead, punctuated by regret.
Not a word says it all
but a part of each next breath says
"thank you."

I think of my parents no more a couple.
My father, dearly departed
along with Thanksgiving dinners
cousins and aunts all around,
the tradition of years,
disappeared from the world when he left it.

It is simple to know that nothing ever lasts,
impossible to live accordingly,
while memory of the lost,
keeps changing. Thankfully.

She sits in a steel and vinyl chair on wheels
in a room reeking
of medicine and old orange juice
in a wilted paper cup.
No reason to open a window
in a room depleted of air and hope.

Occasionally she is dressed
and travelled to the dining hall,
where strangers with no shared history
sit captive in their new-old social club.
Visible and invisible ghosts
make small talk in the air about today,
their shared tomorrow, certain and unmentioned.

I have visited this place
and the body who birthed me
just a fistful of times,
eye on the clock,
as if staying too long,
would swallow me up into the end of time.
As if looking into my mother's eyes,
takes us both back to what we both
can't undo.

In this residence, the past is shadow and the future an abyss.

But what lens of the present
captures wave against cliff?
While the urgency of youth in a game,
disturbs the sand,
oblivious to shoreline erosion.

All we can see is the sea receding,
defying captivity and the ravages of time

decorating wet rocks with
broken glass and shell fragments,
jewels of sea creature corpses,
beautiful leftovers gifted to the living
from oceans of time.

Every footprint is erased
every crime forgiven.
Every century's violence
swept to shore
retreats in the calm of a tide
ebbing back into oblivion's ocean.

All we can do is gaze from the edge
while youth and beauty,
ignorant, and blessed
are lost in the moment
of moon turning tide
and sun sinking to sea,
in the aftermath of Thanksgiving.

"Stereotypes"
Aliya J'anai Granger

I am black...
I can chow down watermelon like a shark in a feeding frenzy.
I can sing gospel with all the riffs and runs possible.
And I can shake my hips and grind if I wanted to.
I am black.
I do NOT like KFC.
I do not admire Kanye West or any other rapper for that matter.
I do not know how to double-dutch.
I am black.
I can speak grammatically correct.
You know, how the "white folks talk".
I am black.
CORRECTION;
I can speak grammatically correct,
You know, as though I've read a BOOK before.
I am black.
I can pop my lips and sway my head.
You know, how "black folks talk".
I am black.
CORRECTION;
I can pop my lips and sway my head,
You know, how black folks THINK they should talk.
I am black.
I can mold to fit into my environment.
I can transform like a chameleon on a hot desert sand.
But I will gasp in the heat of my peer pressure wondering which
group I really belong to.
I can translate slang so the "white folks" can understand it.
I can translate big words so the "black folks" can understand it.
But when I come across a "niggah" that knows more words than I – I
get confused.
And when I come across a white person that speaks worse than any
"niggah" I've ever met I laugh at the walking contradiction and go
about my day.
I don't understand why stereotypes define cultures.
I don't understand why I become "less black" if I get a good grade.
I don't understand why I become a "white girl" if I talk softer and
with less movement.

I don't understand why the stereotypes decided that white people get to be the smart ones.
But most of all, I don't understand why black people agreed.

Moments of Honey and Fire
Nance Reynolds

Morning sun pours light over and under each line,
through the purple of the Jacaranda tree...
reaches gently into each corner of this new world
under each shadow on this street- where we begin.

Pulsing crowds teeming with breath and movement,
eyes and voices, colors and shapes ...
Continuous and unbroken, fitting into spaces
that do not seem to exist.

Moments are suspended – like honey.
Yes, like honey

Sweet, slow, and amber calm, for now.
Suspension shifts, as moments can no longer keep pace.
They lurch forward as my heartbeat abruptly accelerates,
breath catches,
light penetrates.

The amber sweetness is quickly lost
    As I notice – me, white girl.
    Nairobi, Kenya.
No other white girls up and down the street,
Not to be found in corners or under awnings in this new world,
Only the rich, deep stream of black.

Morning sun pours light over and through us, you and I.
Our eyes meet and then dart away, find their way back.
You Black, Me white
Behind our eyes fill with confusion, guilt, loss, pain, anger, awe,
    separation, unity...
    penetrated with the longing of centuries.

We don't know how to fit ourselves into this space,
the search feels like pressing toward a keyhole in the dark,
    seeking passage.
Moments spin and twirl, tumble and stand up again,
Alive, uncertain, orange fire for now.

The teeming crowd moves one way- away,
heart signals despair and also, knowing,
reminiscent of the subways at home – this known and deep ache.
Knowing we met
I wave to you. I wave to you.

Spectrum
Tamiko Lemberger-Truelove

There is nothing between us now
but brooding ether and unfulfilled space.

Words are no longer cargoes of slight dishonors
burgeoning in nascent despair.

What we have made ourselves into no longer
possesses power or distinction in the hollowness
of an indiscriminate gorge. The void does not
acknowledge light or darkness.

You are no longer unsurpassed (unrivaled, incomparable)
becoming no more and no less than a being stranded
in chasms of indomitable grace and ubiquitous obscurity.

Who will I be without scavenged garments clinging to my skin?
Or you, shorn of luggage seeping with history and objects
of mendacities and domination?

What will all of those misapprehensions and fantasies
of colorlessness become now that you are marked
and teeming in hues and shades (as I am),
having been absorbed into the spectrum?
Alas, aberrant one, you must disinter yourself to meet your
humanity.

Climbing Sacramento Street in San Francisco

Paul T. P. Wong

The burden of time
Gets heavier
With each step uphill.

I need to go home
To my tiny home
In this foreign land.

I want to go home,
But where is my home-home,
To which my heart belongs?

I must climb the hill,
Against the gravity of
Age and sorrows –

A thousand sad tales,
Like the Yangtze River
Flowing Eastward....

Where is my homeland?
Where is the laughter
Of children flying kites?

Where is my homeland,
Where neighbors eat together
After a long hard day?

Every cell of mine
Cries desperately for oxygen
And for my motherland.

Shall I lean on my lonely cane,
Or cast my fate into the wind?
Shall I sit down and watch the sunset?

But, my weary soul
Can't find rest anywhere
In San Francisco.

Hunger
Glenn Graves

The poem evokes the pain and hunger of feeling left out and wanting
something that is on the other side of the glass window, or coffee table
or somewhere else, anywhere but here.

Cool breeze moon
Blue neon bright red by the saxophone rhythm of cars
And echoing cafe windows and talk, so much talk
Desert lipped liquored people
Saying something of themselves
To be liked or loved
Or lonely on the street corner
Laughing, looking, listening
Content right there
Over there
Up ahead, just past
Not here
Seeing something strange in the echo of that coffee basin Blu time
With street walking surround sound of Hips and lips and falling hair
And chairs being slid forward and pushed back
To the wall
Of my hunger pang notion of love

Both Sides
Nesreen Alsoraimi

Both sides are consumed by greed
Both are in dire need of revision
Provisions that are too slow to emerge
leave me submerged
in my own purgatory
Feels so lonely
here
Feels so lonely
here
I fidget and fight
I stand behind this faltering light
until it dims
and night takes over
and I hear the resonance
of a vacant stadium
The end does not seem
as tangible
when so few join
when each cause
stands by itself
too far apart
shaking at the knees
Cohesions fail and freeze
little demolitions
and fuzzy thoughts
leave chemical trails in my head
Convincing me
to stay in bed

Generosity
Candice Hershman

Big Daddy Granny,
short and sweet
in faded black Cadillac

pulled up behind me
at the Oakland am pm
and rolled down

the window, flinged
out her tired arm
and displayed her wares.

"Wanna buy some
socks for the boy,
help my grandson out?"

I saw my eyes
in that young black
boy face, shame

and sorrow, poverty
eeking it's way through
the smell of asphalt,

gasoline and urine,
but I have to say,
the socks were clean.

I pulled out my last five,
looked at the boy, and
a whole story was there

existing silently in
the straight line between
his frown and my smile.

I felt myself snagged on
her dignity and his

knowing beyond years,

heart stretched like taffy,
exhaled out a chuckle
in that exchange, but

it's hard to exhale laughter
when reality's just knocked
the wind out of you.

————————————————

This poem is about poverty, although I have to say that it is linked to race. I wrote this when I was providing in-home therapy to families in Alameda County, mainly the city of Oakland. I cannot ignore that nearly every family I visited was black or brown skinned. To me, this points to a correlation of deep concern - the glass ceiling and the collective trauma that manifests in the personal, so often via violence, addiction & poverty. I have not worked there for years, and after reviewing all of my poems, I realized that I have not addressed these issues because while living in Marin County, I have not been exposed to these issues. That speaks volumes.

Gifts of the Least of These
Carrie Pate

Hearing stories
Always learning to listen
    From listening to hope of understanding
        To hope of learning
More stories than
Can fit in a list
    Too numerous though recorded under
        Meaningless numbered codes
    Holding the life of culture, of human
        Suffering and joy
Each beyond
The label- name, rank, serial number, demographic, diagnosis
    That we call differences- that are really experiences
        Told-given- as gifts to listeners
Despite barriers
Of language
    Of traumatic fears, aggressors I resemble
        Without acting or speaking, still listening
Not listener
Not healer
    But receiver of gifts of stories equally
        Ancient and present- human stories
Experiences that
Ought bring tears
    Even nightmares hidden within so-called normal
    Or told in broken English, of losing family for loving the
wrong kind of person
        Being the wrong person
        Being in the wrong place, at the wrong time
        Because of demographic difference
        Searching for voice for justice
            Or understanding
            Or belonging
            Or being
    More than a sex, race, age, religion, gender, sexuality, victim,
      survivor, position, career, party,
        or believer on a never-ending list

                              Because everyone is
something at least
So that when family, society
          Or the self becomes the oppressor
There are still the gifts of connections
          Of real moments
          Of clarity
          Attack
          Rejection
          Venting
          Honesty
          Of finally
                    Being human

My Imperfect Perfect Son
Louis Hoffman

For all those who share in the experience of Trayvon Martin

My imperfect perfect son
Why did you go walking down there
That fateful night?
You know better,
You know the rules.
Why did you wear those clothes?
If you dress like that,
You better be prepared to act accordingly
Why did you get angry?
And why didn't you just submit?
My imperfect, perfect son
Why?
Why are we now left grieving
After so many wrongs?

My imperfect, perfect son
Why did you go walking down there
That faithful night?
You know the rules are different for you
Some freedoms, in this great country,
You still don't have

My imperfect, perfect son
Why did you wear those clothes?
Those innocent clothes
They do not mean the same thing on you
As they do on a white man of
a certain appearance
Though they serve the same purpose
In the chilly night air

My imperfect, perfect son
Why were you so scared?
And why were you suspicious of this man
Who approached you with a gun?
And why did you let these fears and suspicion

Show as anger?
You know your fears will be dismissed
While the aggressor's will be perceived as real
You know your suspicions are not seen as valid
As the man who chose in advance to hold the gun
You know your anger is never seen as justified
Because of the color of your skin
You are just a child,
But you will be expected
To be the bigger man

My imperfect, perfect son
Why did you think you could live in this world
With the freedoms so many others enjoy
Without question.
You were not free, my son
As our freedom is only within
In how we will respond to the injustices
That constitute the world in which we live in

My imperfect, perfect son
Why are we left grieving
Another of so many wrongs?
Another tragedy befallen on
Our community?
But know, my son
That this wrong will not be forgotten
This wrong will inspire
In this wrong we will find our inner freedom
And in this wrong we will speak out
We will scream out
And we will not stop
Until this inner freedom
Is matched
In the world we must live

Note: An earlier version of this poem was published in the January, 2014, Society for Humanistic Psychology Newsletter in an article titled, "Trayvon Martin and Humanistic Psychology: What Does Humanistic Psychology Have to Say About Trayvon Martin?" by Louis Hoffman.

Someday
Yasna C. Provine

My skin,
everyone else's story
so easy to tell,
in a manner that's so predictably wrong,
was my childhood shame.
Dark,
not black,
too black,
not like us,
a raven, too bashful to fly.

I was my mother's Chilean reynita,
the neighborhood's exotic negrita,
a confusing object
with breasts, teeth, and hair of textured questions.

And if I wasn't a thing,
I was no-thing,
invisible,
forgotten,
an ugly duckling.
This lowly opal pigeon,
the strange bird
with a malformed beak,
was thankful for the broken wings
that I could at least hide beneath.

I remember thinking:
Beautiful someday.
Graceful someday.
Treasured someday.

I fell in love with someday.

I would learn to fly there

until someday became part of a distant
point of focus,

so cruelly unknowable,
like the space between sleep and wakefulness,
that disappearing sense of placement
in the scenery of a once perfectly vivid dream,
that space where the heart breaks.

I remember thinking:
There is no beauty in someday,
no grace in someday.
There exist no treasures in someday
for a strange bird
like me.

I perched, tucked my neck in,
balled up under sunset,
drifting under night.
There,
my feathers caught the glimmer of
a black and gold sky.
I saw the galaxy, astonishing and vast,
reflected in every part of me.

I became
boundlessness
and someday disappeared.

Suddenly majestic,
feeling more unique than strange,
and now cosmically divine,
I plucked my feathers and
inked their tips in vessels of poetry.
I assembled my shining opal quills,
dripping with light,
into a crown
of me.

Words lit caves
into nests of truth.
Newly reborn,
I flew out of each one,
not towards the horizon of someone else's someday,

but of belonging
to a shared species of beautifully
broken selves.
All of us, once ugly ducklings,
emerging from time to time to
celebrate that there is no beauty in someday.

There is no someday.

It is now.
I am now.
I am yesterday, too.
I visit but I do not stay.
A sankofa,
I tend to my childhood raven, duckling, and pigeon,
who each still call out to be fed with nurture.
I sing them my songs like a sparrow.
I dance with them as bright quetzals do.
Like an owl, I share wisdom
by quietly watching in trust.
When they tire, they tuck in their necks
and they glow,
dreaming about someday, when they will fly.

A reflection of everything, and everyone,
I am beautiful now,
just as you are, right now,
not someday.

Rain on Me
Joy L. S. Hoffman

There's a wasteland, a wasteland
Where nothing will grow
It's been sucked dry
By the people you know
Once fertile soil with flourishing life
Now broken down to a surface of spite
Beaten, bruised, and scarred from within
Innocence stolen from a childhood friend

Thirst for vengeance
Hunger for justice
Let someone else feel the guilt and the pain
Pour your healing, forgiveness and mercy
Cover me completely in the peace of the rain

There's a wasteland, a wasteland
I just don't know
If someone will love me
Once they know
Withered and scattered, lost to the wind
Desperately seeking the love of a friend
Healing, but terrified of any man
Will I ever trust again?

Thirst for vengeance
Hunger for justice
Let someone else feel the guilt and the pain
Pour your healing, forgiveness and mercy
Cover me completely in the peace of the rain

There's a wasteland, a wasteland
And something will grow
It's been nurtured and loved
By a person you know
Quietly emerging, move with the wind
Learning to find myself again
Validated, respected, healing from within
Showing a glimpse of life again

No need for vengeance
Justice provided
Someone else took on the guilt and the pain
Healing, forgiveness, mercy, and grace
Covered completely in the peace of the rain

Why I Have Grown to Hate Dolls
Nesreen Alsoraimi

Porcelain breasts
Peering at me
Leering at me
The lust painted on
her face
Representing the decay
of warm flesh
and the advent of
Synthetic touch
Counterfeit love
Grasping for handfuls of
fantastical sirens
maniacal contradictions
Feminine and hard
arms just right
on cinched waists
If they are so harmless
why does it gnaw at my core?
Bother me more
than I would ever like to admit?
I'm aware and attend
To what I have been taught to contend with
quietly
rationally
Don't let "jealously" infringe on an otherwise
lovely facade
Dreamy and audacious
Locked in their cages
For art and for beauty
We excuse the prodding
the exploiting
and relish in the woman's body
The feeling's contagious
But it's much more than that
those feelings
those acts
those who create
and those who inundate

themselves with false God
after Goddess
It's all part of the lie
Part of their pitch
Getting a piece of the American pie
To take you from the present
To discount the message
of truth you would feel
if you let empathy heal
the damage they've done
To turn you away
from real live people
the plain and simple
What now seems to pale
in comparison to
a magazine image
That's who will suffer
Not the emotionless doll
Not the face plastered on the wall
So who will you chose?
Who will you love?
Will she be good enough?
To keep yourself up?
Or will you succumb
to the trap that has trained us
to crave instant gratification
and long term alienation
Who will reciprocate?
Will she feel second best?
To an image or celebrity?
Whichever you choose
It will be felt and known
It will override words
and seep through the drone
of the rehearsed song that we sing
Which will it be?
Will you worship your lover?
Or worship their likeness to what you wish they could be?

Where Do Strawberries Come From?
Amara Cudney

A bowl of strawberries
teased me on the sill,
hormone infused
and redly tinted
a color that couldn't have been true.

My greedy fingers
reached for one
 succulent fruit and
 brought this
specimen to my watering mouth.
The aroma of sugar and heaven mixed in vapors of rain.

As red juices ran
down from my lips,
I wondered which
copper colored
child had bent and picked
these heavenly jewels all day
under an angry hot sun whose regard was empty.

Was it a sister,
a brother or both?
Did they sleep on the ground
did they eat each day?
did water seep in their home?
this divine essence I hold in
my mouth. So much richer than a jewel.

Bi the Way
Emily Lasinsky

It has been an exhausting journey navigating the in-between,
Constant questioning, "What the hell is wrong with me?"
Having a category still wouldn't be easy,
Would still be perceived as confused.

As a child, I was called a Tomboy.
This was cute until about 5th grade,
when those in my shared parts tribe started to deny their skills and
talents for the sake of the opposite sex.
Playing sports and climbing trees in cut off tees and long basketball
shorts no longer glamorous,
A year changes everything.

Maybe I would have perceived this shift as less shocking if it
    happened progressively,
Maybe if I had small hills with the hope of developing mountains
instead of the presenting plateaus,
Maybe if nature would have nurtured me a little more.
My mind told me that I was ahead, but my body told me that I
    needed to catch up.
Challenge needed to grow, but this push/pull was debilitating,
I was blooming too late,
I was wrong somehow.

Tried to fight it, but school and home instilled fear,
A heightened state with few things in my control,
Created an environment
for anorexia to bloom.

In-patient, finally part of the in-crowd,
The youngest of 15 starving souls,
Everyone had a plateau,
It was glamorous.
We weren't friends, but empathized with each other's pain. We
provided the therapy.
Gorging until a coma set in, morning sentiments, group, individual
check-ins, weigh-ins, can't even take a piss without eyes peering in,
put the pills in your mouth-check, check again to ensure swallowed,

Ingested the daily bullshit.

15 minute phone calls, I usually made the calls,
Received a call that my family had been in a car accident on their
    way to see me,
Anxiety shot through the roof, but I didn't get to see them,
It wasn't visiting hours.
I became RAGE!
I'm not a freaking criminal!

At 13 years old, I learned that my voice didn't matter,
Did what I needed to do to make the weight, but
Anorexia stayed with me for another 8 years-
Intervention failed.
I guess I didn't try hard enough.

College was an escape,
The first year I turned away from everything I had known and it was
    good,
Not all my choices were great, but the difference was good.
Entered a relationship and quickly became what he wanted me to be,
Talk of marriage and moving in together at age 21,
This is what I wanted, right?

My [he]art told me something different.
All the images of opposites-the push/pull finally being externalized
    in a healthy way,
But I was called bi-polar as a joke.
Convinced that diagnosis was more acceptable than who I actually
    was, and I almost believed it.

But now I understand that some people don't like the ambiguous,
They need to know you are this or that-neither and both are not
    options.
If not a given, they will give you a label,
Yet be a bystander as you cry for help.
My cries weren't the right pitch,
He left with no warning,
Again, something was wrong with me.

At 24, something clicked,
I just didn't care anymore,
Used the past to help me move toward my goals.
The girl dressed in all black with a dog collar necklace,
The girl who suddenly left junior high for the "loony bin,"
The girl who forced an attraction for the sake of pleasing others,
Would one day become a counselor.
Who would have thought?

I still laugh at my chosen profession, but it's a responsibility I take
  very seriously.
I know the hell one can experience trying to express herself,
The fight to be comfortable with one's identity and not become a
byproduct of society.
Being who you are is NOT a mental illness.

Some may dig too much into my words,
Try to psychoanalyze, enforce their meaning between my lines.
For these people circling around and around on your bicycles,
traveling that same path of thought,
I invite you to take off the bifocals of ignorance,
and finally see that
Bi the way-I'm human.

For those who connect with my words,
Nothing is wrong with you.
Tragedy will happen, but each time,
You'll rise.
Don't let one more moment to be yourself pass you bi.

What I Fear

Nathaniel Granger, Jr.

Written in remembrance of Trayvon Martin and those routinely victimized by racial profiling.

Are you so afraid
Of my skin so brown
You use all possible means
To keep me down

Are you so afraid
You have to lock me up
Keep me shackled
Kick my butt

I'm not afraid of you
Let me make that clear
Your baseless fear of me
Is what I fear

Are you so afraid
That I look suspicious
That like a rabid dog
You attack so vicious

Getting autographs
While at the gun show
While your victim marked absent
Another "No Show"

Another Black teen
'Sleep in the mortuary
No remorse, your conscience clean
Evil portuary

I'm not afraid of you
Let me make that clear
Your baseless fear of me
Is what I fear

Are you so afraid
Of the way I talk
You will kill me dead
For the way I walk

Are you so afraid
That I'll take your power
When I simply want to bloom
Like any other flower

By George, I pray
Remove this fear
Before another murder
A mother's graveside tear

I'm not afraid of you
Let me make that clear
Your baseless fear of me
Is what I fear.

I Don't Want To Hate Being A Woman

Candice Hershman

Palm pressed against my brow,
I recline into the part of me
that has never changed -
the little short haired girl
who looked like a boy -
and I feel a failure.
Why is my greatest virtue
what I suspect to be
my greatest womanly blunder?
I remember
my youth pastor loved me
for placing a poem to God
in the collection plate every Sunday.
But the boys never liked me.

Man loves mystery,
and I have none.
If I wear a fan over my face,
I cannot feel the sun on my skin.
I am stranger to the art of geishas,
burlesque queens and maidens.
If I lose a glove, I look for it.
I am not a mystery
because like men,
I seek mystery
and strive to make it plain.
Thus, my voice is plain.
Thus, I am plain.
Plain in my convictions.
Plain in my confessions.
Plain in my generosity.
Plain in my resentments.
Plain in my desire.
I am named for candor.
But in my chest,
my heart beats irregularity,
takes brief intermissions that are inhuman
so that I can be close to death

and every other real thing
that fear builds a bridge to.
My dreams are prescient
and reveal too much,
but the pain is my own mystery,
and rather than be solved by others,
I must solve myself.

This year,
I was called "Midwestern" once again
by several men,
something I used to hear near 20 years ago.
I am not exotic.
I could never wear an embellished mask
over the frames of these glasses
that seek to sharpen my acuity,
see love in the dark
and glean God from clean bones found.
I am not alpha,
will always be the woman
to shy away at the pluming
of other tails that raise
to reveal and seduce.
I am beta.
I surrender.
I do not want to fight that hard.
I hate the game of it,
despise competition,
and would rather be a sister to women
than an enemy.
I have always given up the man.

I read things:
internet published mediocrity
on how to be a woman,
how to please a man,
how to be happy,
how to,
how to,
how to,
and everything opposes

the verity in my soul.
I do not want to lay back in wait
so that I can be found.
I feel rage at the double bind,
fanged in its hunger,
sharp with its rules,
murderer of eros.
To win as a woman,
I must lose at life?
I read my guru books
and tell myself to name it.
This is my task.
To name.
Thus, to be plain.

Mirabai whispers to me:
"this is the price,
as some call it true love,
for you, it is to find true life."
I feel her losses.
Sylvia, Sexton, and Virginia
scratch at my door,
the other side being
the inside of a coffin
that holds everything
I am asked as a woman to bury.
I want, sometimes,
to crawl in with them
and go to sleep,
to be held by them
and tell them I will succeed
in what they gave up on
beyond what they've penned.
I will write and find happiness.
Other times,
I am alone in nature,
with God,
and
I feel joy.
I take a drink of wonder.
My conviction to persevere,

this rises in my heart,
fills in the gaps
of its irregular beating.
I want to be what those women were,
and manage to stay alive.
I want to let go,
be grateful for my early pubescent animus,
and be intimate with everything around me.
I don't want to hate
being a woman.
I want to love
being entirely
human.

I am a Girl
Levia Gee

People criticize me all the time
Some say I complain a lot and
I always have a negative view on life
The truth is I like to suggest something or
Make a counter statement because this is the only way
I know how to let my voice be heard

I am a girl
People say mean things about me
But obviously they don't know anything about me
I just want to sing and dance to my favorite song
So that I can forget all about the gossips in the air

I am a girl
I'm eighteen years old
I've never had a boyfriend and I've never been kissed
I think to myself, "I'm just a filthy, ugly girl"
My family and friends, they all say I'm beautiful
But honestly, I kind of find it hard to believe

I am a girl
I am sweet with a little bit of spicy on the side
There is a time when I'm fun and playful
There is also a time I get real serious
My friends and family teased me about my size
They are so amused by my small size;
Most people describe me as a tiny, short girl
But don't be fooled by my size;
I'm strong and tough like a lion!
Dare try me and you'll hear me roar!

I am a girl
I can't quote the entire Bible
Sometimes I break the golden rule
I am just like everybody else
I fight with my family and friends
But I also have a great love for people
And I'm also a talented girl full of passion

I am a girl
I love to write poems and to sing;
Music inspires me to hope and dream
I have a strong desire to do something great for the world;
To shine the light and bring hope into people
But for now I must set my head straight.
I am a God girl and that's all I'll ever be

Pieces
Stephen L. Granger

Trying to write verse
Spite spurts
I love too much to like Earth
Still hope
Souls will start to feel close
Remove steel cloaks
Speak truth
We bleed blue
Until corruption seeps through
Peace through
Finding pieces of ourselves
That fit together

Pretty Disordered
Nesreen Alsoraimi

Collecting pretty things
Caged birds singing
To a deaf cityscape
Empty milk crate
Head buried under those
1000 thread cotton sheets
Comforted by an advertisement
Comic relief
I sink deep
Whenever my container leaks out
Truths about you
Truths about me
You can't convince me that
It's pathological
Not now, not after I learned what I could
All your false knowledge
And prescription strength powers
Of persuasion
Derailment
Convincing them that they have a disorder
For objecting
Rejecting
Your reality
Then you shoot them up
With chemical solutions
And they wander from then on
In aimless directions
Dependent on you
You, who gave them the poison
When they asked for compassion
Compost piles
Of desperate souls
Unfortunate roles
They play in this
Tragic comedy
Another malady
Pops up in each unmet smile
Each misunderstood child

In dire need of confirmation
Not empty validation
Yes I will confirm
This lie
Yes I will embrace
Your anger
My anger
No it's not alright
They were never all right

Face of Privilege
Louis Hoffman

I am not a strong man
As my success might suggest
I am one whose privilege
Protected me from failure

I am not a giving man
Though my generosity
And empathy are noted by others
I am one who gave
Never having known hunger

I am not a hero
Or champion of the underprivileged
I am one for who it has been easy
And taken accolades I do not deserve

Against Diversity

Tom Greening

It's part of my innate perversity
to remonstrate against diversity.
All others should attempt to be like me
and humbly bow to my authority.
I am the best that anyone can be—
why is that hard for all you dolts to see?
I pity those poor souls who wander, lost,
and are by the daimonic wildly tossed.
They could be saved if they would recognize
that as a guide I am profound and wise.

Becoming
Trent Claypool

Here I sit
Notice me
I am crying out to be seen
But, not too close.

Why won't you look?
I am right here,
I have always been right here.
But, I haven't.

Maybe I am shy?
Perhaps, I must look
Perhaps I need to be here
But, what will I see?

Will I be pleased?
Will I be mortified?
Perhaps, this is pain.
Perhaps, this is beauty.

The Song of Your Life
Paul T. P. Wong

Everyone has a song in their hearts -
A song of hopes and yearnings,
Of endless struggle and heartbreaks.

Don't just whisper your sorrows;
Break out with an explosive voice,
That reaches Heaven and Hell.

Sing, my friend, sing.
Sing with all your heart and all your soul,
Let's hear the song of your life.

Lunch on the Redwood Highway
Amelia Isabel Torres

Just had lunch off the side of the highway
on a little turnout that's so beautiful and comes up so quick,
you'll miss it if you're not looking out for it.

Luckily, it was waiting for me.
The honey bees, the pines, and I all dined together.
They were very pleasant company.

A thought occurred to me as I was eating:
one day my children may read my writing.
Actually, this thought had been forming in the back of my mind
and nudging at me since I started this trip. So, now I realize
I must acknowledge you,
my children.

You are nowhere near being born yet.
I haven't even met your father.
I am simply Amelia,
a 25-year-old free spirit
traveling up the Pacific Coast along the Redwood Highway.

I want you to know how much I love you,
and I don't even know you yet.

I want you to know how much I love life.
I want you to know how amazing I think the world is –
how beautiful and awesome it is.
I want you to know that I am living my life to the fullest
and how I am doing the very best I can
to be a human being
on this earth.

I want you to know that even though you are not here with me now –
I feel your presence.
You're whispering to me on the winds through the pines,
embracing me through the warm sun on my neck.
I feel you here,
you familiar strangers.

The world is an incredible place.
Eagles are soaring.
Crows are laughing,
and cars are passing by chasing their own destinations.

I want you to also know that I have a framed picture of
Jesus with me. I printed him out at work on computer paper
and put him in a light blue frame.
He's been traveling with me, too.
I want you to know that my spiritual journey has been a long one –
it has not always been easy to have Jesus
in my life. Man-made religion corrupted him for me,
and for many years,
I did not wish to acknowledge his presence.
It upset me to even say his name
or hear other people talk about him.
Now, I understand that it was not
Jesus I was angry at
but at the men and women
who perverted his message and his teachings.

I am now working on my relationship with Christ.
And he has been a very patient friend.
I do love him so.

My hope for you,
my children,
is that you can know him, too,
and form your own relationship with him, as well.
Or with Buddha
or Krishna
or Muhammad
or with whomever else you wish.
Because it is through that relationship,
dear ones,
you will find
God.
Source.
The Universe.

Christ is my guru,
my friend,
my teacher,
and through his teachings I am learning to find peace and happiness
in the world –
and more importantly,
within myself.

I hope that wherever you are reading this
that you know how much I loved you
even before you were born.
You are here with me now as I write these words,
just as I am with you as you read them.

Back to the road.
By the way,
I just finished listening to the *Forrest Gump* soundtrack,
and now I've started the *America's Greatest Hits* album.
Ventura Highway is your grandmother's favorite song.

Cereal Milk
Nathaniel Granger, Jr.

*Dedicated to my friend Michael Moats who, while at my kitchen island
collaborating on our book relative to Race and Relationship, paused to
drink with me a strawberry-flavored Boost Protein Shake, to which he
exclaimed, "This tastes like FrankenBerry Cereal Milk!"*

The star struck veil opens
Flannel pajamas warmly reek of last night's dreams
Saturday cartoons
Conjunction Junction
Hooking up phrases, relatives, and clauses.

Breezes affright of Halloween
And twirl the yellow Aspen leaves
The burnt orange Cottonwoods whisper and watch
While Red Maple leaves waltz on the sidewalk
As the Blue Spruce do nothing—Absolutely, nothing.

They are all trees, dissimilar as it may
Outside my window cold
I almost see the white of snow—Taste it
Luring me to my breakfast of innocence
FrankenBerry, Count Chocula; Boo Berry, if lucky.

The bowl as big and round as the world
We sit up close flipping through channels
In the wind Momma's voice echoes
You're going to go blind
I just eat.

Savoring the sweet mixture of what shouldn't be
Slowly drinking the tainted brew
It is well with my soul
Soiled yet pure
Alas, if the world were cereal milk!

I am a Mother

Katelyn Adams

I am a mother
A young mother
A mother of three
I am a single mother
And I am far from rich
I have a fantasy
That thrives with in me
I spend my days fighting
Fighting life
I want to win, I will beat the odds
For if I don't I'll be just like them
One step forward
Three steps back
Nothing's wrong its ok
I'll keep fighting
One day or one way
I'll win or loose
I can see my fantasy
My little home
With my three little people
Everyone is happy
No one has to fight
We have made it
Done at last
Every inch of hope comes an inch of fear
Tired and hopeless it seems
But I am a young mother
And will fight for this
For these three lil' people shall be worth it
Worth the whispers, worth the pain and struggle
In my heart I know our life is not the same
Not the same as the family over there
But if I stay strong maybe they won't notice
I am a mother and I am young but if
I can keep fighting
I will win

Painting by Ted Mallory

The Power of Words
Ted Mallory

Reverend Doctor Martin Luther King Junior wrote that "Injustice anywhere is a threat to justice everywhere" in 1963.

Just last week Nigerian President Goodluck Ebele Azikiwe Jonathan said that "A terrorist attack on any of us is an attack on all of us."

I shared both quotes with my Civics class, but one eighth grader wrote on the board under Dr. King's words that "no one gets this." I asked if they'd like me to discuss it with them and the same student said, "no, we don't care either."

That made me think of Jimmy Buffett's famous line, "Is it ignorance, or apathy? I don't know and I don't care."

I care, God knows I care, but God only knows how I'm supposed to teach eighth graders how to care.

So I took King's words,

Injustice ANYWHERE is a threat to Justice EVERYWHERE

and I paired them with James Madison's words-

We the People of the United States, in Order to form a more perfect Union, establish Justice, insure domestic Tranquility, provide for the common defense, promote the general Welfare, and secure the Blessings of Liberty to ourselves and our Posterity, do ordain and establish this Constitution for the United States of America.

[Disunity] ANYWHERE is a threat to [Unity] EVERYWHERE

[Turmoil] ANYWHERE is a threat to [Tranquility] EVERYWHERE

[Insecurity] ANYWHERE is a threat to [Security] EVERYWHERE

Or would that have sounded better with [Offense] ANYWHERE is a threat to [Defense] EVERYWHERE?

[Suffering] ANYWHERE is a threat to [the General Welfare]
EVERYWHERE!

Now THERE'S one that probably makes "rugged individualists"
absolutely cringe, but AREN'T I my brother's keeper?

And of course,

[Tyranny] ANYWHERE is a threat to [Liberty] EVERYWHERE

So isn't it true?

Don't you CARE?

Don't you realize? Don't you know?

That "Injustice ANYWHERE is a threat to Justice EVERYWHERE!"
Is justice really blind?

Have you ever heard, "No Justice, No Peace!"?

Did you know, what Cornell West says?

He says that "Justice is what love looks like in public."

Merrium and Webster say that "public" means

"exposed to general view :
open, well-known, prominentc :
perceptible, material..."

and

"of, relating to, or affecting ALL the people."

Did you know?

Do you care?

"Injustice anywhere is a threat to justice everywhere"
Amos 5:24

The Jealous Weed that Blooms!
Ronald V. Estrada

Growing up, eyes a rich brown, hair thick and black, contrasting against what looks like a bed of undisturbed mocha beach, my roots reached deeper and deeper into jealousy's soil. I grew up wanting to look like something more appreciated. I grew, believing I was a flower, but being disappointed because as I reached out, life felt more like if I was a weed.

I am a flower, but not the way I know the world prefers. I feel like God was lazy with me, "where are my sky blue eyes and golden hair". I want to be gravitated to. I have had to learn to see myself as magnificent. I have to be convincing before I am seen as approachable.

I've had to dismantle a festering psychology that distorts my vision of self. I take off the devil's lenses, blinding me with superficial facades that taunt my insecurities. I feel, listen, smell, and taste dignity's offerings, and now I can see with grace's luminescence and lucidity. I do bloom!

Growing up my playgrounds weren't segregated, integrated, rather saturated, with brown faces and graffitied up places. I walked there, on dirt paths worn into lush plants that reached out, first grazing, soon biting my ankles and knees, these, these were weeds.

With my socks full of little stickers, tiny hopeful future generations, seeds of weeds, they tacked away at my skin, taking me back, to the witnessing of my uncles tattoo, a mural, on flesh. Christ being tapped into his arm, always gazing out disappointed. On my way to a play area, I wondered, is this what tattoo pain feels like. Mine will be La Virgen on my shoulder.

My playground was a metal graveyard. There were two old banged up animals, staring off into space, being held upright by a metal coil stabbed through their belly, propped in sand. One was supposed to be a horse and the other I guess an elephant. Both were once painted, now chipped and faded. There was a red metal castle, it had a ten foot slide, a round platform, a fire pole through the center, stairs worn to a polished gray. It only takes one time to learn it's too hot to use midday.

I wasn't born racist, I was raised on the basis that there weren't meaningless faces. I wasn't schooled to see equally. My barrios, weren't flower beds, maybe not completely unweeded, but frustratingly somewhere between. I look back and realize, I don't have a vendetta with other races. I was innocent till woven guilty. I was raised in discrepancies, unknown, and now understood honorably as "home". I learned to navigate neglected soils, not knowing different or better. I came from a place I describe as "its all I know". I am a jeal-ist.

I grew into what I thought I was supposed to be, brown. I have held a contradiction for loving most people with an obligation to discriminate. I see that I didn't become racist, I picked and germinated seeds of jealousy.

Jealousy is confusing, igniting my ability to contrast, like when I realized my team didn't have matching jerseys. I had a jersey with number eleven made from tape, a shade of blue noticeably different, stretched and worn from two years past, draping me like I was a hanger for Shaquille Oneal's practice gear. I lost games during warm ups.

Jealousy fuels the longing to be noticed, like when I bought my first pair of stolen Wayfarer Raybans. My jealousy opens up its hard shell using angry desire, the anger necessary to push through enzymes of ambition. I may be a weed but I will grow. Jealousy intoxicated me, disorienting me to deal with sadness impulsively.

Jealousy finally nurtured my anger with unfulfillment. No reward, goal met, or accomplishment was enough. Within the bowels of my germinating jealousy lived the DNA for gluttony, manipulation, and reckless abandon. These qualities were being fed, aligning, and preparing to shoot through the soils of delinquency, inequality, and addiction.

Jealousy created a conflict inside me. Sadly I compared myself to the quality of life shared by a people called whites, they lived in a garden called the heights. I didn't bloom like they do. It started small, like wishing my shoes were different. Then it grew into wasting thoughts about how my pants weren't cool. I sprouted insecurity, seeing and knowing for the first time that I am limited. I began to believe I was something other than a flower.

I still don't consider myself racist. I did grow resentful and have scars that are in the shape of cynicism. The way I look isn't what I believed to be a flower. And the more I look at my surroundings the more I start to see, I look a lot like a weed. My McDonald's didn't have a playground. My basketball courts never had nets. My uncles came home, unlaced layered laces, rung by rung, sweaty and dirty, no tie to loosen. I am longing to be landscaped. When I walk into a room, I see eyes filled with suspicion. It doesn't keep me from walking into rooms. Being a jeal-ist, does not keep me from remembering my roots.

My family loved me like a flower, so that when I learned I might be seen as a weed, it would be enough to sustain me, so I could bloom! I come from a bosque, I am a plant that blooms, unlike a flower, possibly a little jealous. I know that I belong somewhere. I may be called a "weed" in some peoples' yard, but when I bloom, I am flower in someone else's.

The Art of Love
Emily Lasinsky

Together,
Two people who are the same=wrong,
Two people who are different=wrong,
Sets up a predicament of loneliness.

Of course, we could just ignore the norms that society tries to
enforce,
But this really just reinforces ignorance.
These standards, never clearly defined, play a vital role in how we
view ourselves and others.
Fear repercussions if we attempt to cross the bold, thick lines,
Silence our passions and desires,
Miss opportunities to meet beautiful people.

> Step...
> These standards don't sit well with me,
> Love is subjectively defined.
> Created and nurtured by the artists who bring it to life.
> How can an observer tell two people that what they create is
> not love?
> that their colors don't complement each other?
> that finger painting is too messy and a
>   paintbrush
> must be used for love to be born?
> A couple's sexual practices the forefront of the observer's
> mind,
> Never considering that the couple may want to wait until
> marriage.
> Even if this is the goal, they may have to move to another
> state.

This state of mind frustrates me, yet I want to show
compassion to those who may not
understand different expressions of love.
Some may say that they do not agree,
but they will tolerate.
It's a step, but is it enough? No.

Masked hate is not okay.
I am not asking people to change their core belief systems,
   I am asking people to reconsider the quick
                           conclusions they make about others and to
                           concentrate on the heart,
                                  on the art of
                                       Love.

Crowded
Nesreen Alsoraimi

If we could come together
I am not above or beneath you
If we could find that glue
Untapped rivers into truth

I am here alone
In a sea of people
Cyclones traveling around
Pounding on the ground
We've survived a demolition
Been shoved in the wrong direction
This is when stars shine
When uncommon forces align
When they combine
Forming a whole
Feeling control
I want to take this and multiply
By a thousand times
Help young minds fly
And old hands try to pass it on
Ideas that were so far gone

Mainstream miles away
I can barely taste the carbonation
Polished nation
Rotting inside
Borders lined with thorns and
misplaced animals
Were all cannibals
Living off our dying brothers
Enslaved mothers of humanity
Calamity is not so distant
When we are all connected
I am not alone
I'm crowded
Surrounded with leaves of every color
When bridges burn
Lights can dim

How people fade
Faster than I can relate
That's why I'm done looking into empty sockets
Rockets run out of fuel

Everything I own and hold
Has cost the price of someone bought and sold
Every object, every thing
Placed higher than the joy life brings
With every glance and step and thought
Comes the guilt of what's forgotten
With every brand and label sewn
Exploitation is grown
Safe from war and tragedy
Living long and being free
To look the other way
To work so I can pay
For other peoples pain
I'm more callous every day
I've reached new heights
My jacket tight and sights are low
I know

If we could come together
I am not above or beneath you
If we could find that glue
Untapped rivers into truth

Complicit
Louis Hoffman

"The citizens of a city are not guilty of the crimes committed in their city; but they are guilty as participants in the destiny of [humanity] as a whole and in the destiny of their city in particular...."
  ~ Paul Tillich

I sit behind my walls
of privilege
Looking out, seeing the world

A homeless man
is scorned
for having no food
he wanders the parking lot
all he owns left, unprotected
in nearby tent
Yet, he, with no weapon
no threat
is scorned
for making others feel
unsafe
or maybe just
uncomfortable
In SUVs, where
one tank of gas
is a week's nourishment
or one night out of the cold
I sit
I watch
I am silent

I feel the warmth
the dryness
a soft seat
and smooth ride
smelling and tasting
filtered air
snacking on what I don't need
while transporting bag upon bag

of foods of convenience
My comfort is disrupted
by a small group
of tattered tents, followed
shortly after
by one carefully placed
on a small piece of cement
overhanging the road
The owner standing close enough
to be warmed
by the engine of my car
standing at the stoplight
with a sign bearing his
humiliation
smelling, tasting the fumes
of my freedom
He watches for a sign of generosity
courageously overcoming shame
to give me a quick look...
In privilege, I don't look him in the eye

At home
I think I am free
No more reminders to rupture
my comfort
but neighbors now
speak of their scorn
if only a way to be free from this "nuisance"
if only a "pesticide" to take them away
I hear this, to be sure
Yet I am quiet
If I were the voice of compassion
I, too, would be their target
and this, I think, would not be just
I, too, would be accused
for I, had shown them their guilt
I am silent
safe
I alarm my door
and turn off the computer
safely complicit

Longing for the Reclamation of My De-colonized *Indigenous Mind* (A Haiku Series)
Virginia Subia Belton

Spring day with *Colli*   (Grandfather)
Xochitl for my feet, I ask   (flowers)
"Teach me the beautiful words"

Seven years old *Tonaltzintli*   (in the sun)
A shadow covers his face
"No, too dangerous"

Only a whisper
Inin huehue nocol   (This old man is my
He entombs my tongue   grandfather)

Only a whisper
Tahtzintli, my soul comprehends   (Honorable grandfather)
"Your being—danger"

Spring day with *Colli*   (Grandfather)
His garden, my *xochitl* feet   (flowers)
This child is danger?

I bury my tears
With *Inin huehue nocol*   (This old man who is my
Tongue, heart, soul . . . leave me.   grandfather)

I Will Never be One of Them
Heidi Pinson

"Hello" they jeer,
They yell with scorn,
Because their language
Is not my own.

Because the color of my eyes
Is blue and green—but not brown,
My golden hair is far too thin,
My nose—too tall,
It's all foreign.

They think me rich,
And they may be jealous,
Of a facade of a humanity—so called "Western luxury"
That does not exist.

However, I am still not one of theirs,
Too stupid to learn that character language.
They assume me clueless about their culture,
They think "ni hao"—"hello"—I cannot know.

What they know not they will not learn,
That I consider myself one of them.

I love their culture,
Their language, and the characters.
But though I master everything,
They will never consider me one of them.

Breaking My Snow Globe
Nicole Hamlin

Distorted shadows from outside the glass,
The gentle snow falls around me
Safe in my bubble,
Surrounded by my home, my school, my privilege.

The sterile scene of colors dulls with time.
Limited exploration in spite of my ability
The worlds I want to see
Are not held on a map.

Cracked becomes my snow globe
In my quest for education.
Living autumns lining the social spaces:
Colorful garments, colorful people, adornments, beauty.

Discomforts abated by desire,
As stereotypes surface to awareness.
Reflections of subversive socialization
That now hold a repulsive stench.

As pathways to opportunity come to light
I sprint towards them
Because I know that adventure awaits
And they are welcome gifts wrapped in mystery

The globe becomes smaller
And Hungary becomes real.
Budapest in its grandeur of mystery,
Another snow globe, to those about to be encountered.

A privileged education
Opens a pathway into another reality
Something beyond the verbiage of laws,
There are souls buried beneath political rhetoric.

Where there are eyes of children
In an unsolvable maze
Segregation, poverty, and inequality
Barricade their potential opportunities

How long will it take
For the light of equality to shine?
Will it always be blurred
By the clouds of an endless storm?

Within the shadows
The invisible play.
Searching for opportunities
But the darkness is inescapable.

A clock with no hands
Hangs on the wall.
When does time start?
When does it end?

Hope is lost
Waiting for it to change.
When will it come?
Where can I start?

Language was our bridge
Not afforded in its formality.
But with smiles, frowns, pointing, and laughter
Were the primitive treasures traded.

Our limited actions
Afforded a learning relationship
To teach each other new things
Names, games, and things

Sometimes it seemed an unending obstacle
But we learned about each other
Saw the light in our actions
Inviting each other into our lives

Our boundless curiosity
Allowed us to cross boundaries
Of privilege and poverty
And see the strength in all of us

Laughing and dancing in the rain
Or teaching me names and music
Reveals their resilience
To degraded situations

Tourist attractions hold little
Compared to the lived richness of their spirit
They hold onto as they dance and play
While they are fighting their way to the light

Looking from the outside
Tourists may never know
Of the spirit and life oppressed
Just in the shadows beyond

I too, never knew the darkness
Reigning behind the glass
But now I can see a new light
One given to me in the gift of my adventure

My pleasant surroundings of gentle snow
May have shattered on my path
But unexpected treasures bestowed on me
Will change me forever.

Wreckage
Nesreen Alsoraimi

That wreckage
Piles of dust
Sites to dump
Unwanted clumps
Of scattered souls
Battered minds whose bodies stole
That tragic opportunity
To escape the ironic misery
Of a sacred land
In such high demand
On which such menacing plans
Would be drawn
Amidst the olive trees and drumming beats
Of life and love
Walls of deep separation
Construct such odious barriers within a nation
Metal beams falling on stone quarters
Time procreating martyrs
Starting them young
Hardening the human continuum
Then I picture my son
holding that gun
How would I go about
taking it away?
Would I be passive?
Or would I too
awaken a taste for death?
A need for revenge?
A fate romanticized
Lives frozen and nullified
How can I fathom such desperation?
The humiliation
of being a lost people
Deep sense of inferiority
I try
To see you as a person
and not a number
To look into the eyes of every photo

to feel your art
to be a part of your struggle
But I'm here
And I'm safe
And as much as I may read and say
When your writhing in pain
There will be
just a string to connect us
Translucent and weak
Not preventing
Bleak realities

Tomato Picking
Tess Crescini

We climb the metal monster that uproots the tomato plants,
That spits the ripe ones, the green ones, the rotten ones.
We sort them along with the slow snakes and dead rats.
We greet the morning sun from up here.

The clamor of the machine and its ripping,
Shaking loose the ripe fruits,
Stirs a cloud of dust that we breathe
Through the bandanna over our noses,
Fine white dust that settles on our eyelashes and dark hair,
Turn all of us, FOBs and wetbacks, into shapeless grey ghosts.

We speak to one another with our eyes,
Talk about the merciless sun and the endless acres and acres
Of tomatoes yet to be harvested, yet to dumped to the truck
Waiting, grunting black diesel fuel below.

We spend our days speechless, shaken dumb to the core
Until the cool moon rises, spotlights those who walk
As if in a dream, whose tiredness, not even sleep,
Long sleep eases.

Tired of Men Who Need Muses
Candice Hershman

I don't want to be your muse,
your one of nine fantasies,
removed by infinite degrees of separation,
giving to you the kiss of unreality,
the recognition of illusion
that splits me into unrest
among the other discarded bodies
that some would call your nine lives
of others that failed you, your lost selves
misplaced, like condoms
in a bathroom wastebasket,
piled high when you discovered
that they were simply mortals
that could be disgusted
by this tired cliché that you call
"passion,"
the kind claimed by every man
and oddly,
when they didn't reflect the God back
that you so desperately want to be
as you look outward to horizons
that are no longer horizons when you arrive,
this being the moment when
you discover your own rigor mortis
setting in, so then
you can blame them
for not letting you believe
that it is in them,
but not you.
It's the most irresponsible thing
an artist can do.

Believe that their narrow version of
beauty is
the answer.
They will likely die
choking with your cock in their mouth,
voice amputated with your "vision"

and neither one of you
will be closer to God.
Your art may be fascinating,
but your process will be
the most banal drag through the mud
to grace those rows
of blue frigid lips
lined up like train tracks
that go absolutely nowhere,
your own mouth that grazes them
the worst golden calf of all,
defiling all your sacred cows,
and they dumbly accepting
the blindness of your vows.
They will freeze themselves
into an imitation of art
since they've nothing of value to give,
beautiful zombies
looking for a heart to feed on
and a receptive brain
as a host.
They will make themselves
unreal for you.

Your worship is objectifying,
degrading,
a red herring at best
in exchange for another red herring,
extracting the ouroboros of its own meaning,
replacing it with a shameful barter of
quid pro quo . . .

"Hey Baby,
I'll worship you if you worship me."

No thank you.
I'd rather be my own muse
swallowing my own cock back
into a spine that releases
into the natural Godliness
of my inner kerneled heart unraveling.

I want to see the holy within,
to fill myself up,
to birth babies through my fingertips
that denounce all muses,
you, me, and everything,
and simply honor
how the only thing I need
is to open my eyes
to the agony of roses
and ecstasy of worms.
I want to be the artist,
not the object
that you call subject.
I want to produce something
ungodly,
ubiquitously human,
animal,
and even beyond human.
I don't want to passively be fucked
because you need something beautiful.
I want to have . . .

a real conversation.

I'm divinely human,
too good to be your God.

The Skin You're In
Lisa Vallejos

The moment I saw them
I knew there would be trouble.
Their brown skin
Covered in tattoos
Marks of allegiance
To family,
La raza,
Sports teams.
Children.

They didn't frighten me
Because they were some of
My own.
The only difference
The location & amount
Of ink.
Like me, they played in the water
Laughing with their loved ones
Splashing, frolicking
Basking in the warm summer sun.
Beating the heat
But not the indictment
Of their appearance.

It wasn't a surprise when
They were asked to leave
For splashing
At a water park.
It wasn't a surprise
When the police arrived.
To escort them off the premises
Despite their willingness to leave.
It wasn't a surprise
That men who looked just like them
(Only white)
Splashed away
Unnoticed.

My niece and nephew watched
Old enough to recognize
Injustice
But too young to realize why.
Faced with a choice,
I turned to them & pulled back the curtain
On a truth I hate to expose
But must, for their own
Awareness
Knowledge
Safety.

Telling two children
That the world has a different standard
Different rules
Different expectations
Felt too much like ripping
Their innocence away
Not what I had planned for that day.

I was not surprised that I was
Angry.
I was not surprised that I shed
Tears.
I wanted to scream until my throat
Bled.
To give voice to the pain in my
Heart.

"Beautiful, kind-hearted, precious children-
Beware.
For there will be times where you are
Not judged for your
Intelligence
Beauty
Kindness
Compassion
Musical laughter.
There will be times where you are
Deemed unworthy
Unseen.

Devalued.
Dismissed.
Wronged.
Hurt.
Because of the skin
You're in."

And I wept.

The Talk
Louis Hoffman

For my sons

We have to talk,
my son
No, it's not the sex talk,
that will come
and don't worry,
no one has died
Well, that's not what this is about
But its a talk that I
don't know how to have
and a talk where I
don't know what to say
We have to talk, my son
about the color of your skin

You see, my son, your whole life
we've told you that your skin
is beautiful
that you can be proud of who you are:
white and black
We've encouraged you to treasure
the cultures that shaped you
and that you
have nothing to be ashamed of

But you see, my son, that's only
part of the story
and now you need to know
the rest of the story

My son, the world has not been taught
the wisdom your mummy and I
tried to instill;
it is not yet ready to hear
And the world...
Well, the world
will treat you differently

they will follow you in stores
they will perceive you as suspicious;
any anger, no matter how just,
will be seen as threatening
Some will not want you to date their daughters
no matter how proper
and respectful you are
and people will say things
and these things will hurt,
but they will not apologize
and may even accuse you
of being too sensitive
or dismiss you altogether
At times, my son, you may question who you are
because of this unjust world around you

I fear, too, my son
that I have not been a good role model
My skin is not like yours
and I have often taken advantage
I have not kept my hands on the steering wheel
when pulled over for speeding
I have not shown you what to do
when followed in a store -
it has not happened to me
I have not hesitated to be bold in righteous anger
and I have not told you
that if you do the same,
it will be received differently

My son,
you are living in a world
I do not know
I have tried to learn
but my lessons are not as deep
as the ones you will come to know

Please know, my son, that I have tried
I have tried to change the world
I have tried to make it
so that we would not have to have

this talk
I have tried in my anger
and I have tried in my tears
I have tried with some success
and I have tried with some cost
I have fought and fought
and each time I think of you
I have fought more
But I have failed,
and I failed again
I am sorry

My son, this is a beautiful world
and you, too, are part of that beauty
but it is not the world that I want for you
I don't have the answers
but I will walk with you
for as long as God grants me the grace
to be with you.
I will scream out with your anger
and I will cry with your tears
And though my love was not strong enough
to change the world for you, my son,
know that I will never waver
as you walk this world of tears.

Desperate Times
Paul T. P. Wong

In desperate times of starvation
Our souls are sorely tested –
We either risk our lives for a piece of bread,
Or endure the pain and die an honorable death.

How many young men have died
And seen their homeland on fire,
Just for a chance at a decent life,
Free from hunger and oppression.

(Inspired by a Chinese movie)

Faded Chinese Ballroom

Jason Dias

Outside, the garden
Flourishes under sunlight and humidity,
Well-tended and full of life.
A black butterfly flits past
On some inscrutable errand.
Fish glitter in the pond,
As shiny as the coins
Dropped there for luck or hope of luck.
Inside, the hall
Is filled with mold spores
By a rattling air conditioner
That chatters over a carpet past its prime.
Insects crawl in the curtains
In this ballroom past its time.
Outside the men's room,
A rice bug lies on its back,
kicking feebly; its battle it already lost.
The place is slowly being reclaimed
by the Earth.
Chairs,
Brightly colored in
Chinese sensibility,
Sink slowly back into the ground.
This is a place past its time.
Outside the window we can see
Disrepair reclaiming the roofs.
Inside, the paneling and crown molding are damaged.
Things are stained, shabby,
but full of bygone grace and elegance:
Cherubs who will never age
watch from their painted faces
on the doors.
It is a beautiful place,
An aging friend growing wrinkled
And scarred by time.
Perhaps it will be plowed under soon,
Too old to be popular, but too young yet
For reverence and preservation.

Perhaps this place could be better cared for.
Perhaps some new paint,
Some effort with sandpaper and a hammer,
could reverse some of the entropy here.
But for now, the entropy has its own beauty,
And the neglect is essentially benign.

Cultural Labyrinth
Monica Mansilla

Colors and faces,
People and spaces,
Where am I?

In the labyrinth of the world I travel,
In wondering though I question
Is culture for real?
Or is it an invention to make us feel safe?

Is my culture my strength and my safety?
What would bring me alliance and make me feel home
Or is it my weakness, what you'll use to oppress me
What will bring me harm and steal my proud voice?

Countries and cultures
Habits and language
Are we really different?
Are we really the same?

The color of my skin, my accent... makes me one with you
But what if I shall leave?
Will you claim me as your own, or will you abandon me
To the language of the strangers and customs of the alien land

The color of my skin, my accent... makes me different
But what if I should come to you?
Will you adopt me as your own, or will you reject me?
Would you celebrate my uniqueness or convince me to be you

Look at my eyes
Please, see me...
I am unique,
Don't look at my skin, please pardon my accent
I need you my brother, I need you my sister
Without you the world seems empty and sad

In embarrassment of my beauty, I try to change and fit in
The space in between us seems cruel at the time
Yet merging in oneness defeats my existence
Embrace my sweet accent and look at my heart

In the labyrinth of the world I travel
In questioning mind, I try to find out
Who are you my brother?
Who are you my sister?
Not black and not white, not red and not yellow
Just creatures and bleeding to be humankind
Our culture is beauty, it should bring connection
Our culture is humans, one culture, one heart.

Clear Communications
Dan Hocoy

Blunt words, if any.
Disapproving sighs.
Pompous chuckles.
Averted eyes.

Gnashing hate and furrowed stares.
Or cold indifference with a superior air.

What is it...I don't see?
Unless, of course...the problem is me.

The Nile
Nesreen Alsoraimi

Freedom
Is a joke
Only exists in art
Only in part
Can't start a revolution
In my apartment
I can stew
Over past lives
Knives in the backs
Of bright eyed
Passionate hearted
Rebels and refugees
Strangers and my family
How can my ethnicity, my assigned identity
Be an insult to you?
It swishes around in my mind
Knowing you'll want to find out
Sooner or later
Expecting your subdued rage
In your civilized way
Subtle jabs through
the cracks in my cage
You ask softly
deliberately
It darts from my mouth
With a mischievous pride
Even though I don't hold it too tight
Only identify enough to get a kick
Get a rise
From those who think they can hide
I get anxious and read
The reaction I will see
To that simple word
To that dirty place
You convinced yourself has only one face
My mother would be upset
To see that her efforts
Have failed on us

Are we free here?
No
Psychologically not
Emotionally distraught
But would I rather be fearing for my life?
Maybe that would be more simple
Than being caught
Between words
and gestures
Being taught
to self destruct
That we are animals
Inside I feel like a savage
Scavenging for acceptance
Allowed on the ark
as an afterthought
Allotted a certain degree of freedom
As long as I don't mention my past
You coast
on this river
You boast of your tolerance
Of what you have not yet faced
One thing we have
Is this common place
Floating on the stream
In this dream
Egyptian kings and queens
Living in denial
holding us from miles of
uncharted
depths
unstable steps
living connected
As long as I don't mention our past
Everything should be just fine
Packaged and knotted
classified and filed
Plastered titles and fading smiles

I am the Terrorist
Louis Hoffman

"Obviously, all religions fall far short of their own ideals..."
~ Ernest Becker

I am the terrorist
        with droplets of blood staining my cheek
        curled to bruised rib, crying
        "Allah, protect me, save me"
        hearing,
        "God will punish you"
        As air is jarred from my lungs
        Rhythmically, forcefully

I am the terrorist
        having studied peace
        turn the other cheek
        and only violence when no choices
        remain
        Trust Allah, pray, observe
        Trust Allah, pray, observe

I am the terrorist
        ' tho Christians have their KKK, neo-Nazis
        ordained hate, rage against
        liberal values
        but we have no escape,
        we must be one, fundamentalists
        condemn us all so that our sentence is one
        our plague must be abolished
        for a few who make the same judgment
        of Jews, the US, Hollywood values

I am the terrorist
        My black brothers, called immoral
        unfit to live under white sheets
        and bright flashing torches
        My sisters, cleansing his stain
        spat upon as the devil's temptresses
        dirty from his innocence

My gay brothers and sisters, beaten
laughed at, scorned for destroying marriages
by seeking love, security

Yes, I am the terrorist; We are the terrorists
destroying those innocent lives
of comfortable Christians
Deserved of their hate, for destroying
their comfort, and remembering
God's genocide,
holy crusades, witch hunts
Yes, for this, we are the terrorists

Note: *This poem was written after a dialog with a Christian leader who said the world would be a better place without Islam. It is not intended to suggest anything negative about Christianity or religion in general. Rather, it speaks to the potential for **any** religion or ideology to be distorted and misused in polarized ways to demonize others and cause harm.*

Look Beyond the Surface
Stephen L. Granger

What makes you so different than me
From a place beyond the seas
We both seek peace from distant clashes
Same God, different practice
No more you and I, just we
No thoughts on price of life, live free
Wit and wisdom as our weapons
Shall we build past the heavens
I beseech you brethren, take my hand
Wind worries not of water, nor snow the sand
Can't we learn from ways before
Time should not be wasted more
I hate our faces, I love our eyes
I love discussion, I hate disguise
No perfect lives, the surface lies
In perverse times, convert your mind

A Sunday Morning
Amelia Isabel Torres

I am alive. And You are alive.
And there is a trio of us alive.
By the water.

This is a Sunday morning.
Rich with dustless dust
In our cells and clouding the skies.

We are not here.
We are all over.
The same.

The One Thing
that propels us forward
Always speaks.

Since the birth of time
'til the death of days
Suns will burn and moons will die.

And You exist and so do we.
On a morning
By the water.

Vibrant Beige
Emily Lasinsky

A moth among the butterflies,
frantically flapping-1,000 flaps per minute,
putting every fiber of her being into staying
stationary.

The butterflies,
beautifully bellowing-1,000 notes per minute,
never exhausted from creating their majestic waves,
gentle sounds of peace.

The butterflies flaunt their hues,
blue, purple, green, yellow, and orange.
Already pale and sickly, the moth becomes brown.
Saturated in grease,
Saturated in mockery,
Saturated by hard work,
Trips over her calloused wings.

Twitch, Twitch,
no longer even a flap.
Switch, Switch,
direction-away from the sap,
where she is no longer stuck.

The music cannot be produced,
no matter how much practice
and waiting.
The moth will continue to push, push, push,
but what's needed is a pull,
a pull from the outside,
One who sees beyond the off white,
recognizes the true color in her dull wings,
One who will help her discover the vibrant color that has been there
all along.

She is told that there is always hope,
there is something better,
but she finds it hard to accept that this is not a myth.
Likes her beige wings,
offer protection,
Hates her beige wings,
cause rejection.

Nearsighted, only sees present hurts.
Can't allow herself to believe
that the better will not always go to the butterfly,
and the moth will not always be stuck in the myth-
Color blind.

Revelation
Tom Greening

I must confess I'm not too bright—
that's why I thought that being white
was an outstanding noble feature
which made me a much better creature.
But it turns out that all along
I was mistaken, really wrong.
This revelation was a blow—
how I survived I do not know.
Now I must cook up some new scheme.
to prop up my poor self-esteem.

Reek
Candice Hershman

The smell of tragedy is on my clothes,
stale in the air of grief, and my hair -
emanating dust like a smoking gun,
listening to poverty and silence's tongue,
young woman a mouthpiece medium,
friend left behind in the ghetto
by the dead,
and I endure the scent.

Helping like this, strapping on stoicism
is staring down the barrel, the long eyes
of a rifle.

The dead mother left track marks, adhesive
footprints down three flights of project stairs,
seven year old boy stuck to the "souls" of my shoes:

Mommy was shot in front of the school,
in front of him, in the back of the head
and the blood splattered far into deep time,
defied the distance of city blocks
and the pissmarks of graffiti ownership,
blood more posthumous than spray-paint.

Friend shows me the polaroid.
"See how her love is around me."
The image is tattooed on my brain,
and this: I will keep.

But the rest . . .

I want to scrub horror out of my clothes,
to wring out the sweat and ashes of violence
and rinse it back out to the indifferent sea,
wash deprivation and chaos out of my hair,
pound my shoes together like erasers,

to obliterate the "writing on the wall,"
and recycle it into the graveyard of where
things have a chance to grow, to bloom:

to smell of justice and freedom and love again.

—————————————————————————————-

This poem is about poverty, although I have to say that it is linked to race. I wrote this when I was providing in-home therapy to families in Alameda County, mainly the city of Oakland. I cannot ignore that nearly every family I visited was black or brown skinned. To me, this points to a correlation of deep concern - the glass ceiling and the collective trauma that manifests in the personal, so often via violence, addiction & poverty. I have not worked there for years, and after reviewing all of my poems, I realized that I have not addressed these issues because while living in Marin County, I have not been exposed to these issues. That speaks volumes.

Good Fit
Nesreen Alsoraimi

In my face there's a story
You can drink me in
Or pour me
In a glass that fits
In a place that sits well for you
It's what we do
Neat categories
So many broad strokes and gory details
We take and twist
Can't coexist unless
we see you as the same
we have pass along the blame
Shards of me are now lost
Splinters in someone else's arms
The parts don't make sense on their own
When the whole is something I can't recognize
Why are we at war
with ourselves?
As long as this microcosm
emulates
the world at large
This sure seems
like a makeshift reality
like moral stenography
The only time "them" is "we"
is when we join in this depravity
I don't want to unite that way
Don't want to love you because we both hate
and share an enemy
We have the capacity
For real love, you see
We take in all the worldly gifts
But set this one free
Can't we mend this seam?
Disjointed teams
Folding you up and stamping your face

Writing over the story
We need to resist the pull
Reach for nature's
Full embrace

Painting by Richard Bargdill

One Touch
Richard Bargdill

At a grocery store
Not my part of the city
On the way to a tailgate
Just one minor oversight
This item will take it over the top
Hoot! Hoot! Part-ay

Hmm...
might be the only white person here
What am I here for?
It can't be that important

One touch
To my back pocket
To feel
for my wallet—

Not because it was forgotten
But it may already be
Missing
(Though no one was really near me)
Still there. Whew.

Stupid to be here!
Grab it, pay and get out!
Did

Escaped!
Wait...
Is that me?
[Aching]
*Awakening

Who won
Who played
Probably had fun
Anyway

Memory:
Me?
A racist?

All because of
One touch.

The Rage of Ages
Louis Hoffman

"Get over it"
he yelled, with anger
hidden in privilege and power
"Slavery and racism ended long ago
and I am not to blame
for your misfortune."

Taking the words in
like a whipping, shredding
soft skin and weary muscles —
He was alone in a sea of White
Responding calmly,
with the rage of ages:
"Slavery lives on.
in every prison,
in every hospital,
in every food shelter.
It is not dead."
As the silence overcame the room
he knew he could not be angry.
He was not yet that free.

Pecos Fall
Amara Cudney

The mountain gently fell
Into the town,
Like a Tewa mother dressed
In her Sunday skirts
Colored with red, yellow,
And turquoise ribbons,
Yards of flowered fabric patiently gathered
By hand all summer, the streams water trickles,
Singing its way down her cleavage, reflecting
The Pecos' bluer sky.
Giggling, her eyes crinkled
Children's arms draped outside car windows as
Sunflowers, Poleo and Blue Vervain bowed their heads in greeting,
¿ Hola mis nietos, como estan?
Smoke rose out of yards and lots,
Scented with familiar fragrances that made mouths water.
Pungent chilies, roasting chickens,
Vendors signs said, *for sale.*
Young Brown men strutting,
Looking for young Brown girls, so proud and so angry at everything.
Lingering in front yards along the street.
The soft wind snakes through the canyon, whispering
La Reina Fria se biene.

The Blur
Tamiko Lemberger-Truelove

Dreams of darkness warranted invisibility.
Clarity was the smudge on the wall.

Absent understanding of what it was or
what it meant to be the scar on your finger,
the slope of your nose, or how it would cost me
to sustain the opacity of such a muted existence,

I became the diaphanous shield that you obliviously
peered through to glimpse the hemorrhaging terrain,
irrevocably staining you from the void.

In all of the whiteness I was a blur,
though unknowingly, so too were you.

Road to Mend
Michelle Sideroff

I have been told who I am and who I will be based on race, sex, class,
  and being a minority,
But when I ponder upon myself, I see something different and hold
  my reflection in the mirror.
The pieces of being a Hispanic, a woman, and a poet are all the
  beautiful parts to my majority.
The contrasts of the images are sharpened by the assumed power in
  the projection of fears.

I am not who you believe me to be and I do not know where the
  questions or understanding goes.
The closer I get, the faster the person approaching me or walking
  beside me pace falls.
It is no longer a shared space, but a territory of the socially
  constructed hierarchy of the foe.
Judgments reaching out for my submissiveness, then when I resist,
  labels and names are called.

The sharp pain of tightened muscles spread from my neck down to
  my chest.
High pressure of short and quick breaths among tears held back
  against my eyes.
A loaded silence filled with hurt, fear, and anger surrounds a state of
  unrest.
Turmoil of assumptions, blindness, and judgments continue the tall
  tales of whys.

Stop, stop, this cannot go on. It has to come to its end.
Heresy is forbidden and I fight to move, free, as I am.
Heed the pauses in the battle of judgments to tend.
A permissible creed of discrimination is a competent sham.
I bid bye to the stalemate and contemplate the road to mend.

We all have felt this pain and fear there is no escape, for judgments
  are present every day.
They lurk on the streets as drive-by judgments are muttered in jokes
  or nonverbal pull-aways.

It lives among us at home where poor acceptance, denial, and
ridiculing thrive in the family system.
Society sends messages of identities and conformity that build
internalized racism, sexism, and all -isms.

To the You, I don't know, and the I, you just met, let us talk about our
similarities and differences.
I can deconstruct immediate beliefs I have placed on you when
confronted by your bare humanity.
Now, I listen to you tell me who you are without the worry of power
triggering the masks of defenses.
And humility soothes the scrapes of insensitivities and lessens the
building of misunderstood insanity.

Stop, stop, this cannot go on. It has to come to its end.
Heresy is uncomfortable and I stumble forth, free, as I am.
Heed the discrepancies as you are exposed to new knowledge to
tend.
To an abandoned creed of fostered discrimination, I no longer give a
damn.
I attend to the wounds and welcome the healing toward the road to
mend.

We each have sat in the judger's chair and can change that approach
with questions and respect.
First, know the assumptions that have filtered through based on
stereotypes, stories, and biases.
It is not inhuman that we have them; it is harmful when we hold on
and use them to not accept.
To open the dialogue of discussing identities and to exchange
impacts through safe processes.

Let us foster reframing and confrontation to help us build the bridge
of safe connection.
It may sway in the interactions and learning of cultures and other
times stand strong.
We will push and pull, navigating how you and I shift in the layers
and matrices of tension.
And erase the mythical line of what we assumed was between labels
of right and wrong.

It calls upon each of us to use our voices for ourselves and others
who are being marginalized.
Employ our ears and hearts to empathize and apologize for wounds
we have done to others.
Cultural awareness is a complex and dynamic organism that is
immortal for it is never finalized.
Hope transforms hate into love for all shades of faiths, races,
sexualities, families, and colors.

Stop, stop, acceptance and cultural awareness can go on. It does not
have to be a dead end.
Heresy is encouraged and I walk forth, free, as I am.
Heed my invitations as I offer considerations and responsibilities to
tend.
To a saved creed of garnered acceptance, I very strongly give a damn.
I forgive my wounds and the wounds I have done on the healing road
of mend.

Waking
Carrie Pate

Today I saw my past self, visiting across from me in casual
conversation,
And halfway through I realized myself,
Then wondered if I would go back-
     Where the world was simpler
     Finding amusement at the unfamiliar
     Believing that it was worth thinking that a way might be
        right-
But that thinking began to crack with experience, vicarious and real,
Meeting people and learning truths,
Ever slowly coming into knowing-
     About the subjectivity
     Other ways of thinking can be
     As useful, important, and beautiful as they are different-
When misunderstanding generalizations cast long shadows
Over the emerging newness of my
Own learning and change
     Or the ancient challenge
     Of explaining the world
     Outside of the cave of Plato's pictures on a wall.
Perhaps it would be easier to enter the waking dream,
To go back to sleep and ignore,
Enjoy the luxury of forgetting-
     What's behind the looking glass
     Or outside my own door
     The covering of ignorance and want-
But the truth is the fight is as much mine as any
For what actually limits
The judgments and oppressions-
     Only to a group of "others"
     To which I don't belong?
     Because the truth is, I am as much the other-
And will only become more so through my own fault,
By ignoring the cries and alarm
And simply returning to sleep.

We are More
Dakota Gundy

We are more...
We are more than what people see externally.
We are more than the title of our jobs or career.
We are more than the physical presence on the Earth.
We are Divine Beings.
We are created in God's image.
No person is a mistake
No person is wrong for who they are and how they express
themselves.
We are more than the reality we see in front of us.
We are Divine Beings.
We are more than the title of brother, sister and parent.
We are Sparks of the Divine, who created us.
We are more than we know we are.
We need to remember who we are.
We are limitless.
We are more than our judgments on others and ourselves.
We are more than the labels we have placed on others.
We are divine beings. Remember who you are!
We are keepers of the Earth.
We are to love everyone and everything.
Remember who you are part of the Divine, as is everyone.
For ALL are created in LOVE by Divine Love.
Treat everyone as if they were God standing in front of you, because
they are.
All are created in the perfection of the Divine to express themselves
as individuals here on Earth.
We are more than flesh and blood.
We are more than skin color, race, and ethnicity.
We are more than...
We are Divine Beings.
Remember who you are!
Divine, You are DIVINE.
Don't Forget, You are Divine
As is everyone and everything.

Appendix
Poem Activities

Activity 1: Poems in Different Voices

Divide in groups of 4-6 people, preferably with individuals who represent different forms of diversity. Take turns choosing different poems from the book. After a poem is selected, have everyone read the poem silently. Next, have at least 2-3 different people read the poem, allowing for at least 20-30 seconds of silence between each reading. Do not discuss the poem until after all the readings are complete. After everyone who is going to read the poem has gone, use the following discussion points to guide the discussion. Avoid debating the meaning or implication of the poems. The purpose of this activity is to examine the different meaning and experience that this poem brings to individuals.

1. Each author will bring her or his own interpretation or embodiment to a poem. Discuss what meanings seemed to come forward with the different readings.
2. Have each reader discuss how their own reading felt different than the others.
3. Discuss general reactions to the poems.

Activity 2: If This Were My Poem

Our colleague and pioneer dream researcher Stanley Krippner frequently encourages an approach to dream analysis that can be applied similarly to poetry. When sharing a dream in a group setting, Krippner will encourage people to respond beginning, "If this were my dream..." Applying this to poetry, one could read a poem and then respond saying, "If this were my poem..." Instead of trying to interpret the meaning of the poem, the reader can try to "take on the poem." This activity can be done in by yourself or as part of a group discussion where different participants read or listen to a poem and then respond beginning with, "If this were my poem..."

Activity 3: Writing in a Different Voice

One way of using poetry in the service of empathy is to attempt to write in the voice of another person. Several poems in this volume, including "I'll Drink to Judgment," are examples of this. For this exercise, spend some time trying to get into the experience of someone from a different culture and then attempt writing a poem in their voice. It is important to recognize that we can never know someone else's experience and this exercise is not intended to suggest that we can know what it is like to be someone from another culture through writing a poem in a different voice. However, the process of preparation as well as the process of writing can often bring unexpected insight. The preparation may involve reading stories, watching movies or documentaries, or listening closely to people speak about their experience. Engaging in these activities with the intent of writing in another's voice often changes the way one listens and sees.

Activity 4: Becoming an "O"

As you read the poems, imagine that you were the only "O" (minority) in the midst of Xs (majority). What and how do you feel? What do you want the Xs to know and understand about you? What can we do, as Os and Xs, to embrace the diversity of humanity and create an atmosphere of inclusion? Please watch: A Tale of "O" - https://www.youtube.com/watch?v=p56b6nzslaU

1. After reading *Stay Awhile: Poetic Narratives on Diversity and Multiculturalism*, design a field situation in which you will be a member of a non-dominant group.
2. Think creatively about how you could place yourself in a safe, alcohol free situation where you would be a visible minority, i.e., an "O." Some examples include being a male attending a Tupperware party, a person attending a religious service of faiths very different from your own, etc. Consider:
    a. The situation.
    b. Any special permission, access arrangements, or other special accommodations that will be required for you to enter into the situation in a safe manner that is also respectful of the group you are engaging.
    c. Your plan, including methods and timeline, for obtaining access.
    d. The reason you selected this particular setting.
    e. Your predictions about your reaction to the situation and the reactions you expect from members of the dominant group.
3. Becoming an "O." Do not have a friend accompany you on the field experience.

    a. What did you learn about the group you entered?
    b. What values, beliefs, assumptions are held by the group that is different from yours?
    c. What did you learn about yourself?
    d. If you had to do the exercise again, what would you do differently?

Activity 5: Immersion

Multiculturalism is not easy. If learning to appreciate diversity and becoming culturally competent were as easy as reading a book, listening to a lecture, or taking a course, we would not have many of the problems that are so evident in the world today. Multiculturalism and diversity are topics that need us to stay awhile, sometimes in uncomfortable places.

If you read a poem from this book a day, it would take you over 2-months to complete. Even if you have already read the book once, we encourage you to make a commitment to read through this book once again at a slower pace. As you read through at this slower pace, try reading 1 poem a day. As you do this, here are a few suggestions to enhance and deepen this journey:

1. Read the same poem 2 or 3 times a day, including once at the beginning of the day and once right before going to bed. These times are important. Reading the poem in the morning can help you to be mindful of the meaning this poem can bring to you throughout the day. Also, your unconscious will continue to reflect upon the poem even as your consciousness is directed to your daily routine and responsibilities. You continue to process information at night in your sleep Reading the poem again before bedtime primes your unconscious again to continue processing the poem.

2. In at least one of these readings, read the poem out loud.

3. With each reading, take at least 3-5 minutes to reflect upon the poem, its emotions, what it evokes in you, and what it might feel like to be the author or voice of the poem.

Editor Biographies

Louis Hoffman, PhD, is a faculty member at Saybrook University and Director of the Existential, Humanistic, and Transpersonal Psychology Specialization. He also teaches courses in Saybrook's Creativity Studies and the Consciousness, Spirituality, and Integrative Health Specializations. Dr. Hoffman teaches two courses on poetry: Poetry, Healing, and Growth (Once a year this course is open to individuals not enrolled at Saybrook) and The Use of Poetry with Death, Loss, and Life Transitions. An avid writer, Dr. Hoffman has five previous books, including *Existential Psychology East-West* and *Brilliant Sanity: Buddhist Approaches to Psychotherapy*, as well as numerous book chapters and journal articles. In recent years, the use of poetry to promote healing and changes has become a more prominent theme in his writing and scholarship. For many years, Dr. Hoffman has written and incorporated poetry into his teaching and professional presentations. Dr. Hoffman is Past-President of the Society for Humanistic Psychology (American Psychological Association, Division 32). He is a Licensed Psychologist in Colorado and California. Throughout much of his career, he has maintained a private practice offering therapy, assessments, and supervision in addition to his academic work. He lives with his wife, three sons, and his dog, Dante, who serve as a continual motivation for his poetry and writing.

Nathaniel Granger, Jr., PsyD is a Licensed Minister, practicing psychotherapist, author and poet, transformational speaker, and executive coach. He has been published in *The New Existentialists* and *Journal of Humanistic Psychology* and has a twenty-five year span of working in Human Services. Nathaniel is a graduate of the University of the Rockies (formerly Colorado School of Professional Psychology) where he received a Doctorate Degree in Clinical Psychology with a specialization in Forensics. He also received a Masters Degree in Counseling and Human Services and Bachelors Degree in Psychology from University of Colorado at Colorado Springs. He has received several awards and scholarships for demonstrated scholarly excellence and dedication to the field of psychology; with particular interests in Existential/Humanistic Psychology relative to diversity and human dignity. Incidentally, Dr. Granger is originally a product of the inner-city, where gross poverty and dropping out of high school facilitated in succumbing to life on the streets of Chicago, where he received Life's proverbial degree in "hard-knocks." However, through perseverance and determination, enlisting in the U.S. Army and beginning his formal educational pursuits at the community college level, he has since served in many capacities in the arena of Human Services to include but not limited to Director/Founder and Pastor/Psychotherapist at Be REAL Ministries, Inc. in Colorado Springs, Colorado; Professor of Psychology at Pikes Peak Community College, Colorado Springs and Adjunct Faculty member at Saybrook University in Oakland, California as part of the Existential, Humanistic, and Transpersonal Psychology Specialization and Transformative Social Change Specializations as well the PhD Clinical Psychology Degree Program. Dr. Granger currently serves as Secretary on the Executive Board of the Society for Humanistic Psychology (American Psychological Association, Division 32). His embodiment of Dr. Martin Luther King, Jr. and reenactment of the "I Have a Dream" speech, along with his oratory gifts that gives life to any topic, has rendered Dr. Granger a desired and sought after speaker. His energetic love for humanity is passionately exemplified and warmly accepted, and his doctoral dissertation, "Perceptions of Racial Microaggressions among African American Males in Higher Education: A Heuristic Inquiry," along with *in vivo* experiences, and interests in Civil Rights are the substrata upon which a majority of his work in academia, writing, and public speaking is predicated.

Other Books by University Professors Press
www.universityprofessorspress.com

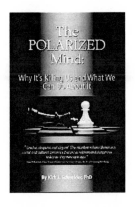

The Polarized Mind:
Why It's Killing Us
and What We Can Do
About It

by Kirk J. Schneider

Bare:
Psychotherapy Stripped

By Jacqueline Simon
Gunn
With Carlo DeCarlo

An Artist's Thought
Book:
Intriguing Thoughts
about the Artistic
Process

By Richard Bargdill

CPSIA information can be obtained
at www.ICGtesting.com
Printed in the USA
FSOW01n2336050115
4363FS